意味&使い分けが**見る見る**わかる!

ピクトで学ぶ
英会話必須単語

ソ・ヨウンジョ著

3000+

JN087430

はじめに

「私は夕食を食べてからSNSをチェックする」という文を、英語ではどう言うでしょうか?

「今日、久しぶりに掃除機をかけたよ」という文はどうでしょう?

難しい単語は一つもないように見えますし、日常的に会話で使う文ではありますが、いざ英語で表現しようとすると、適切な単語やフレーズが浮かんでこない!そんな人も多いのではないでしょうか。

『ピクトで学ぶ英会話必須単語3000+』は、まさに、そのような方々のための本です。

会話の基本は単語

会話の基本は単語にあると一般的に言われています。単語が集まって文になり、単語があってこそ意味を伝えることができるからです。例えば「私の目は一重まぶただ」という文を英語で言う場合、「一重まぶた」に当たる英単語を知っていなければなりません。「現金で支払います」という文を英語で言うには、「現金」という英単語を知らなければなりません。このように、話したいことを伝えるためには、その意味に該当する単語を知る必要があるのです。

日常よく使う単語を知ることが大切

それでは、どのような単語をどれだけ知っていればいいのでしょうか?

オックスフォード英語辞典には、30万を超える単語が収録されているそうです。そうは言っても、私たちはこの多くの単語をすべて覚えることはできず、覚える必要もありません。英語が母国語でない私たちは、自分に必要な単語だけを知っていればいいのです。日常会話のために、metaphysical(形而上学の)やsubconscious(潜在意識の)というような単語まで覚える必要はないですよね。自分の日常や関心事、周囲で起こることを描写するために必要な単語を知っているだけで十分です。

会話の必須のフレーズも紹介

しかし、必要な単語をたくさん知っていれば自然と会話がうまくなるわけではありません。私たちは一つひとつばらばらの単語で話をするのではなく、単語をつなぎ合わせてフレーズを作り、そこから、文を作って話すからです。例えば、「地下鉄に乗ります」と言いたい場合、「地下鉄」、つまりsubwayという単語を知っているだけでは不十分です。「地下鉄に乗る」という意味のフレーズ、つまり、take a subwayを知らなければならないのです。「あの銀行のアプリをインストールしました」と言うためには「アプリ」、appを知っているだけでは不十分です。「アプリをインストールする」という意味の、install an appというフレーズを知らなければなりません。

この点を考慮し、本書では単語ばかりでなく、単語を含む意味のかたまりであるフレーズも紹介しています。両方合わせ3000以上。それらを使った例文も掲載しているので、会話ですぐに活用できます。

時代に合った単語とフレーズを知ること

私たちが生きる今の時代は、固定電話よりもスマートフォンが一般的になり、街の商店での買い物と同じくらい、オンラインショッピングや海外からの個人輸入が日常的になりました。そのような時代の変化に合わせ、本書では最新の英単語とフレーズを紹介しています。1日の日課や衣食住、仕事、健康管理はもちろんのこと、インターネットショッピングや個人輸入、スマートフォンとSNSの利用、男女平等や福祉など各種の社会問題や環境問題に至るまで、21世紀に生きる私たちが日常でよく交わす話題を網羅し、各テーマにおいて特によく使われる表現を収録しました。

本書を1冊勉強したからといって、ネイティブスピーカーのように話せるようにはならないと思います。しかし、この本の内容を自分のものにしてしまえば、いつどこで外国人に会っても、物おじすることはないでしょう。楽しく豊かな会話を交わすことができるはずです。

みなさんの英語生活を応援しています。

春を待ちつつ
ソ・ヨウンジョ

単語を話すだけでも意思疎通はできる！

AさんとBさんの2人がいます。2人とも英語、特に会話を上達させたいという強い思いがあります。そして、会話の基本は単語ということで、単語学習を一生懸命しています。どのようにしているのか、見てみましょう。

A 私は会話の基本は単語だと考え、会話に使えそうな単語をメインに勉強しました。専門的な単語より、日常でよく使う単語を中心に。そして、単語ばかりを勉強したわけではありません。学んだ単語が使われている会話の文章を丸ごと暗記しました。その結果、外国人と話す機会があったときに、適切な単語と自然な文章で話ができました。ですから意思疎通は以前よりも楽になりました。今では英会話に少しずつ自信がついてきています。

B 私は学生時代からの習慣どおりに単語を勉強しました。1日に30単語ずつ覚えるんです。英単語と日本語の意味を対にして。そうすれば理論的には1年に1万ほどの単語を覚えられることになりますが、実際には、ひと晩寝ると多くても5個くらいしか記憶に残っていませんでした。そして、せっかく苦労して覚えるのならば、という思いから、難しい単語をメインに勉強しました。しかしそのような単語は、いざ外国人に会って会話するときには、ほとんど使い道がありませんでした。だから、目いっぱい苦労はしたものの、会話の実力はひとつも伸びていない状況です。

皆さん、どうですか？
会話を上達させるためには単語をたくさん覚えなければならないと思いながら、会話では決して使うことがないような単語ばかり勉強し続けてはいませんか？
会話が上手ということは、自分の考えと周りの状況をしっかりと伝えられることであり、そのためには、まずは自分の周辺で目に入るものを英語で表現できなければなりません。重要なのは、このような目に入るものを英単語で表現することなのですが、多くの人の単語学習は、学生時代の試験対策のための英語学習法から抜け出せずにいます。
本当に英会話がうまくなりたいならば、もう一度単語の勉強から始めてください。ネイティブスピーカーと出会って話をするとき、お互いの関心事や日常の出来事について話すことが多いでしょう。だとすれば、これに合わせて単語の学習法も変えるべきです。さらに単語学習の利点は、差し迫った状況においては、文章ではなく適切な単語やフレーズだけでも意思疎通ができるという事実です。
単語の学習をしっかりしなければいけないと思えてきましたね？
それならば、数多くの単語学習書の中で、なぜ『ピクトで覚える英会話必須単語3000+』で学習するべきなのでしょうか？

この本で勉強すべき決定的な理由！

1 こんなにも多様なテーマの単語だなんて！

前のページにも書いたように、外国人に出会ったら、私たちは主に「日常と関心事」について話します。ただ、一口に「日常と関心事」と言っても、その範囲は非常に広いのです。この本ではそれを大きく16の章（＝大テーマ）に分け、その章をさらに多くて10、少なくて2、平均5つのUnit（＝小テーマ）に分け、必須の単語とフレーズを紹介しました。スマートフォンや地球環境問題など、最近の生活、社会に合わせた最新の語彙ももれなく紹介しています。

2 こんなにも使い道のあるフレーズだなんて！

好ましくない英単語学習法とは、「英単語⇒日本語の意味」という形式でのみ英単語を覚えることです。もちろん、このような形で覚えていい単語もあるにはあります。しかし、この本では、単語を個別に紹介するだけではなく、会話で多用される単語の集まり、フレーズも数多く紹介しています。例えば「拍手をしましょう！」と英語で言いたい場合、「手」→handを知っているだけでは不十分です。「拍手をする」→clap one's handsというフレーズを知る必要があります。「うつ伏せになれ！」と言いたければ、「うつ伏せになる」を意味する英語フレーズ、lie on one's faceを知っていなければなりません。本書では、すぐに会話で使えるよう、このようなフレーズを幅広く紹介しています。

3 こんなにも素晴らしいイメージだなんて！

人間の脳は、文字だけを覚えるより、文字とイメージを同時に覚える方が、記憶に定着すると言われています。これを活用し、単語・フレーズを最大限効果的に記憶できるよう、この本ではピクトグラムなどのイメージを一緒に掲載しています。イメージと合わせると、単語の意味が頭の中により鮮明に残るでしょう。また、イメージを見る楽しみもあるので、単語学習が苦になりません。

4 こんなにも的確な会話文だなんて！

宝の持ち腐れという言葉どおり、単語もフレーズも文にして初めて、実際の役に立ちます。この本には、「ああ、この単語は英語でこう言うのか」「こういうときはこんなフレーズを使えばいいのか」「自分の場合はこう表現すればいいんだ」と思うことができる、英会話の例文を多数掲載しています。

では、このように素晴らしい構成の本書を、どのように活用すれば効果満点になるでしょうか？

この本の使い方

CASE 1

「本は必ず最初から読むべき！」という人

本を買ったらとにかく最初から順番に勉強していく方たちがいます。そうしないと、何かを学び損ないそうで落ち着かないんですよね。それが必ずしも間違っているとか悪いというわけではありません。特にこの本は、自分自身の話から自分の周辺、さらには社会や国家・地球へと、テーマが徐々に広がっていく構成なので、最初から少しずつ勉強する人にはぴったりの構成です。

本を開くと、ページの上段には、そのページで学ぶテーマと関連して英語のネイティブスピーカーがよく使う単語・フレーズが、ピクトグラムなどのイメージと共に掲載されています。このとき、意識的に日本語を先に見てから、英単語・フレーズは何かを考えてみてください。その上で、自分が思った英単語・フレーズが合っているか確認してください。単語学習にはこの過程が重要です。英単語・フレーズを確認したら、ダウンロード音声で発音を確認し

2

次に、ページ下段のUSEFUL SENTENCESを学習しましょう。ここでもやはり、まず日本語を見て、英語でどう表現するかを考えた上で、英文を確認してください。簡単な文でも、いざ英語で話そうとすると、言葉に詰まってしまうことが少なくないということに気づくと思います。この本に掲載した文は、実際の会話にすぐ使えるものばかりです。こちらもやはり、ダウンロード音声でネイティブスピーカーの発音を聞いてみてください。でも、聞くだけはダメ！　ネイティブスピーカーの読み上げの後を追う形で、自分も読み上げてみてください。数回繰り返すとさらにいいですし、できれば、丸ごと覚えてしまうのもいいでしょう。

表記事項の説明
［ ］は直前の単語と置き換え可能
e.g. send[transfer] money（送金する）は send money と transfer money の2つの表現が可能です。
（ ）は該当する単語を含めて読んでもよい
e.g. all day (long)（一日中）は all day とも all day long とも言えるという意味です。
また、ICU(intensive care unit)のように、略語の後ろに来る括弧は単語そのものを説明しています。

CASE 2

「どうして絶対に最初から読まないといけないの？」という個性派の人

本は必ず最初から読まないといけないという決まりがあるんですか？
いえ、そんな決まりはありません。最初から読み進めないと後半が理解できないという本でない限り、読みたいページから読んでいいんです。特に、この本のような英単語学習書の場合、なおさらです。興味を感じたChapter、面白そうに見えるUnitから始めるといいでしょう。しかし、この場合でも以下の学習法は守ってください。

てください。発音を間違えてしまうと、ネイティブスピーカーでも理解できないため、正確な発音を学ぶことが必須です。

1

3

左ページの下段には（時には右ページの下段）、日本語では意味が似ていても、ニュアンスが違う単語を比較して説明したり、日本人が間違って使っている表現を正しく解説したりしています。上段に掲載された単語から派生した表現も紹介しています。「物は言いよう」は英語においても同様です。ネイティブスピーカーのように完ぺきに把握するのは困難ですが、思いがけない誤解を招かぬよう、必ず知っておくべき事項をまとめました。

/は後ろに来る共通の単語につなげて読む
e.g. the first/second/third/only childは、the first child（1番目の子）、the second child（2番目の子）、the third child（3番目の子）、the only child（ひとりっ子）を表します。

また、/は語句を区別する場合にも使われています。e.g lightning 稲妻 /thunder 雷

Contents

【音声のダウンロードについて】

※パソコンでダウンロードする場合
以下のURLで「アルク・ダウンロードセンター」にアクセスの上、画面の指示に従って、音声ファイルをダウンロードしてください。
URL：https://www.alc.co.jp/dl/

※スマートフォンでダウンロードする場合
以下のURLから学習用アプリ「booco」をインストールの上、ホーム画面下「探す」から本書を検索し、音声ファイルをダウンロードしてください。
URL：https://www.booco.jp/

CHAPTER

1

必ず知っておくべき単語＆フレーズ

Words & Phrases
You Should Know

自分を紹介する表現

`DL 01_01`

was born in
〜に(で)生まれた

age
年齢

**birthdate,
date of birth**
生年月日

birthday
誕生日

**Chinese zodiac
signs** 干支

the Year of the Rat/
Ox/Tiger/Rabbit/
Dragon/Snake/Horse/
Sheep/Monkey/
Rooster[Chicken]/
Dog/Pig[Boar]

子年／丑年／寅年／卯年／辰
年／巳年／午年／未年／申
年／酉年／戌年／亥年

family
家族

**family
background**
家庭環境

**the first
/second
/third
/only child**
(兄弟の中で)一番目／
二番目／三番目／
一人っ子

zodiac signs 星座

Capricorn/Aquarius/
Pisces/Aries/Taurus/
Gemini/Cancer/Leo/
Virgo/Libra/Scorpio/
Sagittarius

やぎ座／みずがめ座／うお座
／おひつじ座／おうし座／ふた
ご座／かに座／しし座／おと
め座／てんびん座／さそり座／
いて座

USEFUL SENTENCES

1987年に岡山市で生まれました。	I was born in 1987 in the city of Okayama.
戌年生まれです。	I was born in the Year of the Dog.
三人兄弟の二番目です。	I am the second (child) of three children.
小さなバイオテクノロジー企業で働いています。	I work for a small biotech company.
血液型はRH+のO型です。	My blood type is O Rh positive.
独身です。	I am single.

nationality
国籍

hometown
地元の町

gender
性別

male
男性

female
女性

**job,
occupation**
職業

**do ~ for
a living**
仕事は〜をしている

**work
for[at, in]**
〜で働いている

work as
〜として働いている

blood type
血液型

height
身長

weight
体重

**marital
status**
配偶者の有無

married
既婚

single
独身

国籍を表現する

国籍は Japanese（日本）、Korean（韓国）、Chinese（中国）、French（フランス）、Indian（インド）
など形容詞形で表現します。

例：**My nationality is Japanese(=I am Japanese).** 国籍は日本です（＝日本人です）。

職業を尋ね、答える

職業が何かと尋ねる一般的な表現は、What do you do for a living? です。このような質問をされた
ら I am 〜.（職業は〜です）、I work for[at, in]〜.（〜で働いています）、I work as 〜.（〜として働い
ています）と答えればよいです。

宗教を表現する

「宗教は〜です」と言うときは、普通 I am a Catholic. のように、その宗教の信者を表す名詞で言います。
I am Catholic. のように同じ単語を形容詞として使うこともできます。どちらも意味は同じです。

Christian キリスト教徒（の）   **Catholic** カトリック教徒（の）
Protestant プロテスタント（の）   **Buddhist** 仏教徒（の）
Hindu ヒンドゥー教徒（の）   **Muslim** イスラム教徒（の）

UNIT 2 時間を表す表現

DL 01_02

1日の時間を表す表現

in the morning/afternoon/evening 朝／午後／夕方に
at dawn 夜明けに **at sunrise** 明け方に
at sunset 日没時に **at night** 夜に
at noon〔midday〕 正午〔真昼〕に
at midnight 真夜中〔午前零時〕に
all day (long) 1日中

頻度などを表す表現

always いつも → **usually** 普通、たいてい → **often** しょっちゅう →
sometimes, occasionally 時々、たまに → **seldom, rarely** ほとんど～しない →
never まったく～しない
* **regularly** 規則的に、定期的に

early 早い、早く **late** 遅い、遅く

USEFUL SENTENCES

ケンジは毎日夕方にジョギングをします。	Kenji jogs in the evening every day.
君は1日中、いったい何をしているんだ？	What the hell are you doing all day (long)?
私たちはよく田舎にドライブに行きます。	We often go driving to the countryside.
最近K-POPが世界的にとても人気です。	K-POP is popular all over the world these days.
今は忙しくて話をすることができません。	I am too busy at the moment to talk with you.
いつかその男性を見た覚えがあります。	I remember seeing him one day.

過去	現在	未来
once upon a time 昔	**these days, nowadays** この頃、最近	**someday** 未来のいつか／ある日 (とき)
a long time ago ずっと前	**this year** 今年	**in the future** 未来に
in the past 過去に	**this month** 今月	**next year** 来年
last year 昨年	**this week** 今週	**next month** 来月
last month 先月	**at the moment** 今	**next week** 来週
last week 先週	**right now** 今 (すぐ)	**in an hour** 1時間後に
an hour ago 1時間前		

* **one day** 未来や過去のいつか／ある日

* **sometime** (過去や未来の)いつか

late vs. lately

late は「遅い」という形容詞としても、「遅く」という副詞としても使われます。「遅く」を lately と勘違いすることがありますが、lately は「最近」というまったく別の意味の単語です。

sometime vs. sometimes

sometimes は「時々、たまに」という意味で、-s を付けない sometime は「いつか」という意味です。
例：Let's go skiing sometime. (いつかスキーに行きましょう)

once upon a time

once upon a time は「昔、昔々」という意味で、昔話や古い話を始めるときに使います。

DL 01_03

three days ago 3日前に	the day before yesterday おととい	yesterday 昨日	today 今日	tomorrow 明日	the day after tomorrow あさって

for the first time 初めて at the beginning of ～が始まったときに	in the middle of ～の途中に、～している途中に	for the last time 最後に at the end of ～·が終わるときに

USEFUL SENTENCES

おとといヒロシに会ったんじゃない？	You met Hiroshi the day before yesterday, didn't you?
人生で初めてローラーコースターに乗りました。	I went on a roller coaster for the first time in my life.
ゆうべ、真夜中に目が覚めました。	I woke up in the middle of the night last night.
彼らは週単位で給与をもらっています。	They are paid weekly.
30年くらい前、この辺りに住んでいました。	I lived in this neighborhood about three decades ago.

hourly 1時間ごと(の)　　**daily** 毎日起こる、日々の、毎日

weekly 毎週の、毎週、週単位で　　**monthly** 毎月(の)、月単位で

yearly 年ごとにある(する)、毎年　　**annually** 1年に1回

biweekly 隔週の、隔週で

bimonthly 隔月の、隔月で

JANUARY	FEBRUARY	MARCH
APRIL	MAY	JUNE
JULY	AUGUST	SEPTEMBER
OCTOBER	NOVEMBER	DECEMBER

decade 10年　　**century** 世紀、100年

millennium 千年

solar calendar 太陽暦　　**lunar calendar** 太陰暦

leap year うるう年　　**leap month** うるう月

every を使う表現

every ～ 〜ごと

every other[second] day/week/month 2日／2週／2カ月ごと

every two days/weeks/months 2日／2週／2カ月ごと

1回、2回、3回〜

once[twice, three times] a day 1日に1回／2回／3回

once[twice, three times] a week 1週間に1回／2回／3回

once[twice, three times] a month 1カ月に1回／2回／3回

yearly vs. annually

yearlyは形容詞と副詞のどちらとしても使われ、annuallyは副詞としてだけ使われます。

例：**This is a yearly event.** (形容詞) これは年中行事です。

例：**They hold the event yearly.** (副詞) 彼らはその行事を毎年行います。

例：**The event is held annually.** (副詞) その行事は毎年行われます。

位置、方向を表す表現

`DL 01_04`

位置

beside ～の横に
next to ～の隣りに
by ～の横に、沿いに

behind
～の後ろに

in front of
～の前に

beneath
～の真下に

under, below
～の下に

on
～の上に、～に

over, above
～の上に

**on the
right/left**
右側／左側に

**on the
right/left of**
～の右側／左側に

on the opposite side of
～の向かい側(反対側)に

**between
A and B**
AとBの間に

**in the middle
of**
～の真ん中に

among
～の間に

inside
～の中に

outside
～の外に

on the corner
隅に

USEFUL SENTENCES

彼らの別荘は川沿いにあります。	Their villa sits by the river.
人々がその店の前に集まっています。	People are gathered in front of the store.
書店は道を渡った所にあります。	The bookstore is across[on the opposite side of] the street.
道に沿って桜の木が植えられています。	Cherry trees are planted along the street.
50メートルくらい真っすぐ行って右に曲がってください。	Go straight about 50 meters and then turn right.

方向

toward(s)
〜の方へ、〜に向かって

across
〜を渡って、横切って

into
〜の中に

out of
〜の外に

through
〜を通って

along
〜に沿って

turn right
右折する

turn left
左折する

go straight
直進する

go upstairs
上の階に上がっていく

go downstairs
下の階へ下りていく

---

under, below, beneath

- under: (特定の物体や層を成す物) の下、(年齢が) 〜以下
- below: (垂直にある2つの物体のうち) の下、(温度／数／量が) 〜以下 [未満]
- beneath: (つながっている状態) の下

例：**Children under 18 can't see the movie.** 18歳以下の子どもはその映画を見られません。

例：**Write your answer below the line.** 線の下に答えを書いてください。

例：**The ship sank beneath the water.** その船は水の下に沈みました。

on, over, above

- on: (ある物の表面) の上に
- over: 〜の上に、(移動する動きを表すときや量・年齢などが) 上回って
- above: 〜の上に、(最低値や固定された数値を) 超えて

例：**There was a picture on the wall.** 壁に絵が1つ掛かっていました。

例：**The dragonfly is flying over the plant.** トンボが植物の上を飛んでいました。

例：**Mount Everest is 8,848m above sea level.** エベレストは海抜8848メートルです。

数／量を表す表現と数の読み方

DL 01_05

数が多い、多数の	量が多い、多量の
many	much
a (large) number of ~	a large[great, huge] amount of ~
a lot of ~	a lot of ~
lots of ~	lots of ~

数が小さい、若干の	量が少ない、若干の
some いくつかの	some 若干の
a few いくつかの	a little 若干の
few ほとんどない	little ほとんどない
a small number of ~ 少数の~	a small amount of ~ 少量の~

USEFUL SENTENCES

多くの人が毎年この島を訪れます。	A large number of people visit this island every year.
インターネットには膨大な量の情報があります。	There is a huge amount of information on the internet.
数分だけ時間をください。	Give me just a few minutes.
もう少し寝させてください。	Let me have some more sleep.
お金が少ししか残っていません。	We just have a little money left.
午後ケーキを少し食べました。	I ate a small amount of cake this afternoon.

大きな数字の読み方

1,107	one thousand, one hundred and seven
12,345	twelve thousand, three hundred and forty-five
762,815	seven hundred and sixty-two thousand, eight hundred and fifteen
2,053,724	two million, fifty-three thousand, seven hundred and twenty-four
15,000,000	fifteen million
550,000,000	five hundred (and) fifty million

序数の読み方

32nd	thirty second
84th	eighty fourth
103rd	one hundred and third
201st	two hundred and first

分数、小数の読み方

1/2	a half
1/3	a third[one-third]
1/4	a quarter, a fourth[one-fourth]
1/5	a fifth[one-fifth]
3/4	three quarters[three-fourths]
1/8	an eighth[one-eighth]
0.2	(zero) point two
1.5	one point five
4.37	four point three seven

日付の読み方

| 4月1日 | April first[the first of April] |
| 10月23日 | October twenty-third |

電話番号の読み方

| 02-987-6543 | zero[oh]-two, nine-eight-seven, six-five-four-three |
| 010 8765 4321 | zero[oh]-one-zero[oh], eight-seven-six-five, four-three-two-one |

ホテルの部屋番号の読み方

| 902号 | nine oh two |
| 315号 | three one five |

5 天気と気象を表す表現

DL 01_06

warm, mild
暖かい、温和な

sunny 晴れた
hot 暑い

cloudy 曇った

rainy
雨の

stormy
嵐の

cool
涼しい

windy
風の強い

snowy
雪の降る

cold 寒い
freezing 凍えるほど寒い

USEFUL SENTENCES

早く暖かくなるといいな。	I hope it gets warm soon.
日本の夏はとても暑くて湿気が多いです。	Summer in Japan is very hot and humid.
曇った天気が好き。	I like cloudy weather.
雨の日はセンチメンタルな気分になる。	I feel sentimental on rainy days.
今日の気温はセ氏氷点下17度だって！	Today's temperature is minus 17 degrees Celsius!
霧のかかった日は運転に気をつけないと。	You should be careful when you drive on a foggy day.

temperature 温度
(minus) ~ degrees
(Celsius/Fahrenheit)
(セ氏／カ氏) (氷点下) 〜度

humidity
湿度

humid
湿気が多い

dry
乾燥した

frosty
霜の降りた

foggy
霧のかかった

天気を表す名詞→形容詞

sun（太陽）→ sunny   cloud（雲）→ cloudy
wind（風）→ windy   rain（雨）→ rainy
storm（暴風雨）→ stormy   snow（雪）→ snowy
frost（霜）→ frosty   fog（霧）→ foggy

セ氏（Celsius）とカ氏（Fahrenheit）

日本をはじめとする大部分の国が使っているセ氏は、水が凍る温度を0度、沸騰する温度を100度とし、その間を100等分して表示する温度。スウェーデンの物理学者セルシウスが考案し、英語で〜degrees Celsiusと書きます。

一方、米国とヨーロッパの一部の国で使用するカ氏は、水が凍る温度を32度、沸騰する温度を212度とし、その間を180等分して表示する温度。ドイツの物理学者ファーレンハイトが考案し、英語で〜degrees Fahrenheitと書きます。

（カ氏 − 32）÷ 1.8 ＝ セ氏
（セ氏 × 1.8）+ 32 ＝ カ氏

6 事物を描写する表現

DL 01_07

大きさ、長さ、重さ、高さ、距離、深さなど

tiny とても小さい → **small/little** 小さい → **big/large** 大きい → **huge** とても大きい、巨大な

short
短い

long
長い、長さが〜の

---

high
高い、高さが〜の

low
低い

---

heavy
重い

light
軽い

USEFUL SENTENCES

この靴は私にはちょっと小さい。	These shoes are a little small for me.
そこは世界一大きい電気自動車の会社です。	It's the world's biggest electric car company.
あそこに、以前、とても大きい木がありました。	There used to be a huge tree there.
東京で一番高い山は雲取山です。	The highest mountain in Tokyo is Mt. Kumotori.
かばん、重いでしょ？ 持ってあげようか？	Isn't your bag heavy? Do you want me to carry it?
その箱、軽いから私にも運べます。	The box is light enough for me to carry.

fat 太った			**slim** 細い、すらりとした
near 近い			**far** 遠い、遠く、〜ほど離れて
deep 深い、深さが〜の			**shallow** 浅い
wide (幅や面積が)広い			**narrow** 狭い

USEFUL SENTENCES

ここから一番近い郵便局はどこですか？

Where is the nearest post office from here?

家から会社まではどれくらいの距離ですか？

How far is it from your house to your office?

この小川は浅いから入って遊んでも安全です。

This stream is shallow, so it's safe to go in and play.

パリのシャンゼリゼ通りは長くて広い道です。

The Champs-Élysées in Paris is a long and wide avenue.

狭い道を運転して通るのはとても大変。

It's so hard to drive along a narrow path.

状態

new
新しい

old
古い、古びた

bright
明るい

dark
暗い

hot
暑い、熱い

cold
冷え冷えした

clean きれいな、清潔な
tidy, neat
整頓された、端正な、
すっきりとした

dirty
汚い

USEFUL SENTENCES

彼女の新しい小説読んだ？	Have you read her new novel?
この通りには古い家がたくさんあります。	There are lots of old houses on this street.
暗いところで本を読むと目に悪いんだって。	They say reading in the dark is not good for the eyes.
このスープ、すごく熱くて飲めないよ。	This soup is too hot to eat.
ジムの部屋はいつもきれいで整頓されています。	Jim's room is always clean and tidy.
汚い運動靴、洗って。	Please wash your dirty sneakers.

loud
うるさい

quiet 静かな、平穏な、口数が少ない
silent もの静かな、沈黙した、音のない
still 静かな、動きのない

hard
硬い、しっかりした

soft
柔らかい

rough
粗い、表面が滑らかではない

smooth
すべすべした、表面が滑らかな

strong
強い、力が強い、頑丈な

weak
弱い、力がない

tough
丈夫な、頑丈な、
強靭な

USEFUL SENTENCES

静かな場所で仕事をするのが好きです。	I like working in a quiet place.
彼が現れると、全員が黙りました。	As he showed up, everyone became silent.
静かな川ほど深く流れる（ことわざ）	Still waters run deep.
この化粧水を塗ると肌がとてもすべすべになります。	This lotion makes your skin feel very smooth.

quiet, silent, still
- quiet: 静かだが多少の音はする状態、心が穏やかな状態、閑散とした状態を指し、口数が少ない人に対して使います。
- silent: まったく音がしない状態、沈黙している状態、発音されない音（無声）を指します。
- still: 動きがなく、もの静かな状態を指します。

6

色

white 白色(の)	**black** 黒色(の)
red 赤色(の)	**orange** オレンジ色(の)
yellow 黄色(の)	**yellow green** 黄緑色(**yellow-green** 黄緑色の)
green 緑色(の)	**dark green** 深緑色(**dark-green** 深緑色の)
blue 青色(の)	**sky blue** 空色(**sky-blue** 空色の)
navy blue 濃紺色(**navy-blue** 濃紺色の)	
violet すみれ色(の)	**purple** 紫色(の)
pink ピンク色(の)	**gray** 灰色(の)
brown 茶色(の)	
beige ベージュ色(の)	**cream** クリーム色(の)
silver 銀色(の)	**gold** 金色(の)

USEFUL SENTENCES

大雪が降ったので、どこもかしこも真っ白です。	It's white everywhere since it snowed a lot.
春の黄緑色の葉がとてもきれいです。	Yellow-green leaves in spring are so pretty.
濃紺色のスーツを着て面接を受けに行きました。	I went for a job interview wearing a navy-blue suit.
「パープルレイン(紫色の雨)」という歌があったけど、紫色の雨ってなんだろう?	There is a song called "Purple Rain". What is purple rain?
彼女は灰色と黒色の服ばかり着ます。	She only wears gray and black clothes.
このクリーム色のブラウス、あなたによく似合ってます。	This cream blouse looks good on you.

wood 木、木材
wooden 木製の

metal
金属(製の)

glass
ガラス(製の)

plastic
プラスチック(製の)

paper
紙(製の)

fabric
繊維

leather
革(製の)

rubber
ゴム(製の)

USEFUL SENTENCES

木製の箸は軽いので使いやすいです。	Wooden chopsticks are light so they are good to use.
金属製のトレーが欲しいです。	I'd like to have a metal tray.
ルーブル美術館の前には大きなガラスのピラミッドがあります。	There's a big glass pyramid in front of the Louvre Museum.
プラスチック製の袋はできるだけ使わないようにしないといけません。	We shouldn't use plastic bags if it's possible.
コンサートで人々が紙飛行機を飛ばしました。	People flew paper planes at the concert.
この革のかばん、重くて持てません。	I can't carry this leather bag since it's too heavy.

7 事物を評価する表現

amazing, awesome, excellent, fantastic, wonderful 素晴らしい、すてきな、立派な
annoying, irritating いらだたしい
boring 退屈な
comfortable 心地よい、快適な、気楽な(↔ **uncomfortable**)
convenient 便利な(↔ **inconvenient**)
dangerous 危険な
disappointing 残念な
disgusting とても嫌な、不快な
exciting わくわくする、興味津々の
frightening, scary 怖い
fun 面白い、楽しい

USEFUL SENTENCES

その映画はとても退屈でした。	That movie was so boring.
この椅子、すごく楽。	This chair is so comfortable.
このロボット掃除機はとても便利です。	This robot vacuum cleaner is very convenient.
選挙の結果がとても残念です。	The results of the election are quite disappointing.
あの男の言葉遣いはとても不快だ。	The man's language is too disgusting.
私は怖い映画が見られません。	I can't watch scary movies.

funny おかしい、笑える
important 重要な
pleasant 気分のいい、快適な、楽しい(↔ **unpleasant**)
satisfying 満足な
strange おかしな、見知らぬ
terrible むごたらしい、ひどい
useful 役立つ、有益な(↔ **useless**)

harmful 有害な(↔ **harmless**)
interesting 面白い、興味深い

shocking 衝撃的な、呆れる
surprising 驚くべき
terrific とても良い、立派な、すてきな

USEFUL SENTENCES

あのシットコム、本当に笑える。	That sitcom is really funny.
サプリメントの摂り過ぎは、健康に害を及ぼす可能性があります。	Taking too many food supplements can be harmful to our health.
あのレストランの料理はとても満足いくものでした。	The meal at the restaurant was very satisfying.
今日、すごく衝撃的な話を聞きました。	Today I heard a very shocking story.
あの俳優の演技はひどかった。	The actor's performance was terrible.
こんな役に立たない物、どうして買ったの？	Why did you buy this useless thing?

8 気分と体の状態

DL 01_11

気分

delighted, glad, happy, pleased
うれしい、楽しい

angry, furious
腹立たしい

annoyed, irritated
いらいらした

anxious, worried 心配な、不安な
blue, depressed ゆううつな
disappointed 失望した
embarrassed 困惑した、恥ずかしい

nervous 緊張した、神経質な
stressed ストレスに苦しんでいる
upset 気を悪くした、心が傷ついた

satisfied
満足な

surprised
びっくりした

USEFUL SENTENCES

それについてあまり心配しないで。	Don't be too worried about it.
ここ数日、ゆううつな気分でした。	I've been feeling blue for days.
彼の反応にはがっかりしました。	I was disappointed with his reaction.
手持ちのお金がなくて恥ずかしい思いをしました。	I was embarrassed because I had no money with me.
私は緊張すると爪をかみます。	I bite my fingernails when I'm nervous.
最近とてもストレスに苦しんでいます。	I'm so stressed these days.

well 健康な、体調がよい
healthy 健康な
strong 強い、丈夫な

unhealthy 不健康な
weak 弱い
ill, sick 病気の

tired 疲れた
exhausted とてもくたびれた、疲労困ぱいの
burned-out 極度に疲れた、燃え尽きた

USEFUL SENTENCES

今日は体調があまりよくありません。	I don't feel well today.
ありがたいことに、うちの子どもたちはみんな健康だ。	Thankfully all my kids are healthy.
彼女は子どもの頃から体が弱かった。	She has been weak since she was a child.
病気のときは薬を飲んで休んで。	When you are sick, take medicine and get some rest.
今日は働き過ぎたのですごく疲れました。	I overworked today and now I'm exhausted.
彼、燃え尽きたんだ。休息が必要だ。	He is burned-out. He needs some rest.

wake up
目覚める

get up
起きる

wash one's face
顔を洗う

shave
ひげをそる

take a shower
シャワーを浴びる

wash one's hair
髪を洗う

dry one's hair
髪を乾かす

brush[comb] one's hair
髪をとく

brush one's teeth
歯磨きする

floss one's teeth
デンタルフロスで歯間を磨く

USEFUL SENTENCES

彼女は毎日2回シャワーを浴びます。	She takes a shower twice every day.
寝る前に髪を乾かした方がいいよ。	You'd better dry your hair before going to bed.
歯磨きした後にいつもデンタルフロスで歯間を磨きます。	I always floss my teeth after brushing them.
化粧するのに5分しかかかりません。	It only takes me five minutes to put on my makeup.
私たちは朝食を取ってから出勤します。	We go to work after having breakfast.
毎朝8時に地下鉄に乗ります。	I take the subway at eight every morning.

put on (one's) makeup
化粧する

get dressed
服を着る

eat(have) breakfast
朝食を取る

have coffee/tea
コーヒー／お茶を飲む

take the bus/subway
バス／地下鉄に乗る

drive to work
車で出勤する

go to work
出勤する

wake up vs. get up
- wake up: 眠りから覚める
- get up: 寝床から起き上がる、座った状態・横になった状態から立ち上がる

歯の手入れ
- brush one's teeth: 歯磨きをする
- floss one's teeth, use dental floss: デンタルフロスをかける
- use an interdental brush: 歯間ブラシを使う

eat[have] lunch
昼食を取る

take[have] a break
休憩する

finish work
仕事を終える

**leave[get off] work,
leave the office,
leave for the day**
退勤する

work overtime
残業する

cook[make] dinner
夕食を作る

eat[have] dinner
夕食を取る

USEFUL SENTENCES

会社の食堂で昼食を食べます。	I have lunch at my company cafeteria.
普段は何時に退勤しますか？	What time do you usually leave work?
最近はあまり残業しません。	I don't work overtime often these days.
私は1週間に3、4回スポーツジムで運動します。	I work out at the gym three or four times a week.
夕食を取ってから、私はSNSをチェックしたりテレビを見たりします。	After eating dinner, I check social media or watch TV.
姉は毎晩入浴します。	My sister takes a bath every night.

watch TV
テレビを見る

listen to music
音楽を聴く

work out (at the gym)
(スポーツジムで)運動する

**surf[browse]
the internet**
ネットサーフィンをする

**check
social media**
SNSをチェックする

**read a book/
magazine**
本／雑誌を読む

take a bath
入浴する

go to bed
就寝する

eat, have ＋食事

「朝食／昼食／夕食を食べる (取る)」という意味を表すときは、動詞eatとhaveのどちらも使えます。ただし、ある特定の食べ物を「食べる」と表現するときはeatを使うのが一般的です (haveを使うこともあります)。

退勤する

「退勤する」は、leave work、get off work、leave the office、leave for the dayなどで表現できます。finish workも使えますが、この表現は「退勤する」という意味よりも、単に「仕事を終える」という意味合いが強くなります。例えば、在宅勤務で仕事を終えたときはleave workではなくfinish workがふさわしいですよね。

SNSをチェックする

日本では通常SNSと言いますが、米国、カナダなどの英語圏ではsocial mediaという用語が一般的に使われています。ですから、「SNSをチェックする」は、たいてい"check social media"を使います。具体的にcheck (out) one's Facebook/Twitter/Instagram (フェイスブック／ツイッター／インスタグラムをチェックする) と言うこともできます。

10 家事

DL 01_14

cook[make] breakfast/ lunch/dinner

朝食／昼食／夕食を作る

set the table

食卓の準備をする

clear the table

食卓を片付ける

wash[do] the dishes

皿洗いをする

separate trash

ごみを分別する

take out the trash

ごみを出す

clean the house/ room/bathroom

家／部屋／浴室を掃除する

clean up one's room/desk

部屋／机を片付ける、整理する

vacuum the floor

掃除機をかける

sweep the floor

掃き掃除をする

mop the floor

床にモップをかける

USEFUL SENTENCES

食事したらすぐに皿洗いをします。	I wash the dishes right after I eat.
ごみ出しをするのは一番上の子の仕事です。	Taking out the trash is my eldest child's job.
1日おきに掃除機をかけます。	I vacuum the floor every other day.
家事の中でアイロンがけが一番嫌い。	I hate ironing the most among housework.
私がほぼ毎日、犬を散歩させてます。	I walk my dog almost every day.
1週間に2回ほど食料品の買い物をします。	I do grocery shopping about twice a week.

**do the laundry,
wash the clothes**
洗濯する

**hang out
the clothes**
洗濯物を干す

**fold
the clothes**
洗濯物をたたむ

do the ironing
アイロンがけをする

iron ~ ～にアイロンをかける

make the bed
ベッドを整える

**change
the sheets**
シーツを替える

**water
the plants**
植物に水をやる

**feed the pet
/dog/cat**
ペット／犬／猫に餌をやる

walk the dog
犬を散歩させる

do the shopping
買い物をする

**do grocery
shopping**
食料品の買い物をする

家事
「家事」はhousework、household chores、「家事をする」はdo housework、do household choresと表現します。

grocery, groceries
grocery(store, shop)は食料品と雑貨を販売する店を指します。スーパーマーケット（supermarket）とほぼ同じ意味です。groceriesと言うと、食料品と雑貨を指します。

2

人

___

Human

人の体 (1)―外部：体全体

DL 02_01

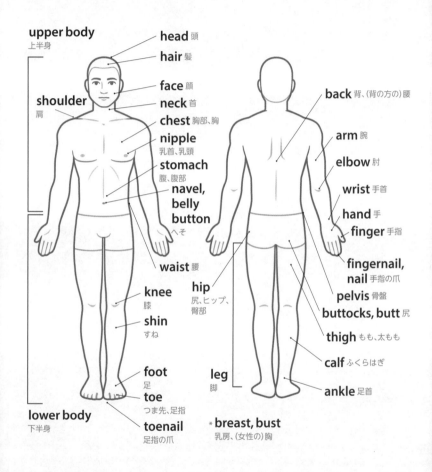

upper body
上半身

head 頭

hair 髪

face 顔

shoulder
肩

neck 首

chest 胸部、胸

nipple
乳首、乳頭

stomach
腹、腹部

**navel,
belly
button**
へそ

waist 腰

knee
膝

shin
すね

foot
足

toe
つま先、足指

toenail
足指の爪

lower body
下半身

hip
尻、ヒップ、
臀部

leg
脚

back 背、(背の方の)腰

arm 腕

elbow 肘

wrist 手首

hand 手

finger 手指

**fingernail,
nail** 手指の爪

pelvis 骨盤

buttocks, butt 尻

thigh もも、太もも

calf ふくらはぎ

ankle 足首

* **breast, bust**
乳房、(女性の)胸

USEFUL SENTENCES

母は下半身が上半身より弱い。	My mom's lower body is weaker than her upper body.
私は下半身太りです。	I am overweight in my lower body.
年を取るほど下半身の運動が大事になります。	Exercising your lower body gets important as you get older.
その男性は肩幅が広い。	The man has broad shoulders.
うつ伏せになってください。	Lie on your stomach, please.
その男性は手の指が細くて長い。	The man has long, thin fingers.

chest vs. breast, bust

chestは、男女を問わず、胸の部位、胸部を指します。一方、breastとbustは女性の胸、つまり乳房を指します。

waist vs. back

waistとbackはどちらも「腰」と訳せるため、判断しにくいかもしれません。waistは胸とお尻の間のくびれた部分を指し、backは腰も含めた背中全体を指します。lower backで「腰」を指すこともできます。

hips vs. buttocks

hipsとbuttocksは、日本語ではどちらも「尻」と訳されますが、hipsは腰と脚がつながる骨盤の部位を指し (前から見える部位)、buttocksは座ったときに席や床などに触れる肉のある部位を指します (後ろと横から見える部位)。つまり、私たちがふだん「お尻」と言っているのは、buttocksに相当します。

2 人の体 (2)―外部：顔、手、足

DL 02_02

顔 **face** 顔

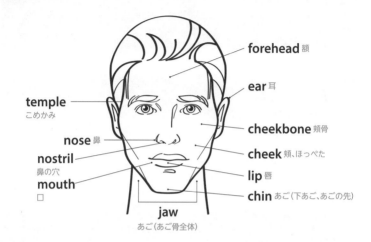

forehead 額

ear 耳

temple
こめかみ

cheekbone 頬骨

nose 鼻

cheek 頬、ほっぺた

nostril
鼻の穴

lip 唇

mouth
口

chin あご（下あご、あごの先）

jaw
あご（あご骨全体）

目 **eye** 目

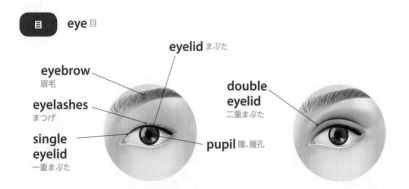

eyelid まぶた

eyebrow
眉毛

**double
eyelid**
二重まぶた

eyelashes
まつげ

**single
eyelid**
一重まぶた

pupil 瞳、瞳孔

歯 **tooth**（複数形 **teeth**）歯、歯牙

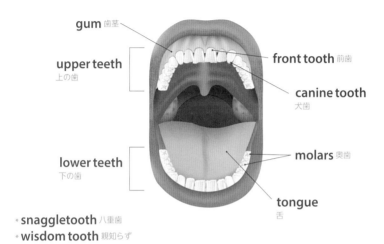

gum 歯茎

upper teeth
上の歯

front tooth 前歯

canine tooth
犬歯

lower teeth
下の歯

molars 奥歯

tongue
舌

* **snaggletooth** 八重歯
* **wisdom tooth** 親知らず

USEFUL SENTENCES

彼は額が広い。	He has a wide forehead.
私はいつも唇が乾燥しています。	My lips are always dry.
その赤ちゃん、まつげがすごく長い。	The baby has very long eyelashes.
一重まぶたの目が好きです。	I like single eyelid eyes.
奥歯に何本か虫歯があります。	I have some cavities in my molars.
親知らずを抜いたことある？	Have you ever had a wisdom tooth taken out?

手 **hand** 手

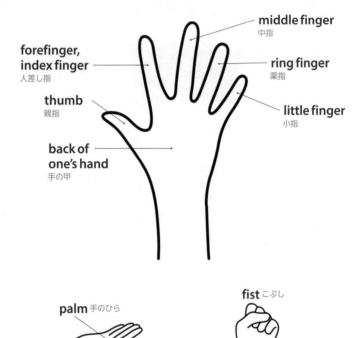

middle finger
中指

**forefinger,
index finger**
人差し指

ring finger
薬指

thumb
親指

little finger
小指

**back of
one's hand**
手の甲

palm 手のひら

fist こぶし

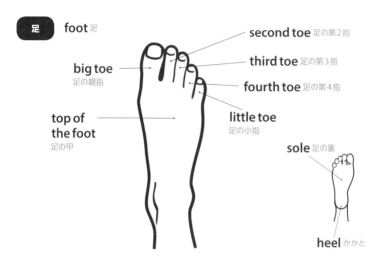

足 **foot** 足

second toe 足の第2指

third toe 足の第3指

big toe
足の親指

fourth toe 足の第4指

little toe
足の小指

**top of
the foot**
足の甲

sole 足の裏

heel かかと

USEFUL SENTENCES

指輪は普通、薬指にはめます。

その男性は手の甲で額の汗をぬぐった。

手のひらに彼の電話番号を書きました。

足の第2指が足の親指より長いんだね！

蚊が足の裏を刺した！

We usually wear a ring on our ring finger.

The man wiped the sweat off his forehead with
the back of his hand.

I wrote down his phone number on my palm.

Your second toe is longer than your big toe!

A mosquito bit the sole of my foot!

3 人の体 (3)—内部

DL 02_04

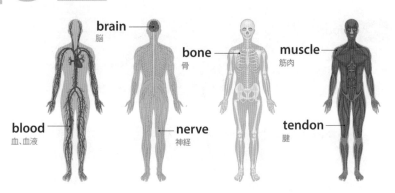

brain 脳

bone 骨

muscle 筋肉

blood 血、血液

nerve 神経

tendon 腱

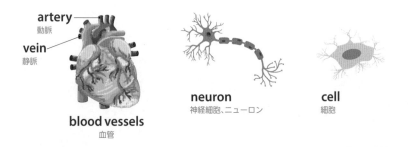

artery 動脈

vein 静脈

blood vessels 血管

neuron 神経細胞、ニューロン

cell 細胞

USEFUL SENTENCES

筋肉を鍛えなきゃ。	I have to exercise my muscles.
のどが痛くてうまく話せません。	I have a sore throat and I can't speak well.
うちの犬は生まれたときから心臓が弱い。	My dog has had a weak heart from birth.
肝臓が弱いと疲れやすい。	If your liver isn't good, you'll get tired easily.
祖母は膝の関節が悪くて手術を受けました。	My grandmother had surgery on her knee joint since it was so bad.

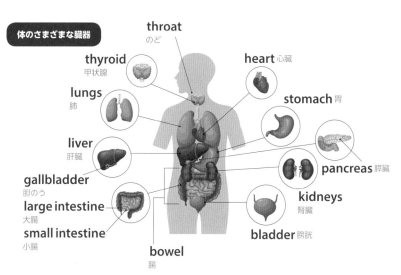

体のさまざまな臓器

throat のど

thyroid 甲状腺

heart 心臓

lungs 肺

stomach 胃

liver 肝臓

pancreas 膵臓

gallbladder 胆のう

large intestine 大腸

small intestine 小腸

kidneys 腎臓

bladder 膀胱

bowel 腸

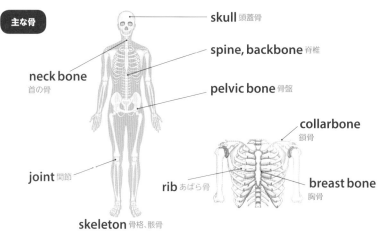

主な骨

skull 頭蓋骨

spine, backbone 脊椎

neck bone 首の骨

pelvic bone 骨盤

collarbone 鎖骨

joint 関節

rib あばら骨

breast bone 胸骨

skeleton 骨格、骸骨

体のさまざまな分泌物

tear 涙	sweat 汗	saliva 唾液
phlegm 痰	eye mucus, sleep 目やに	earwax 耳あか
urine, pee 小便	feces, excrement, stool 大便	

4 体型、スタイル

DL 02_05

short
背が低い

medium height 中背(の)
average height 平均的な背(の)

tall
背が高い

slim, slender
細い、すらりとした

skinny, thin
がりがりに痩せた

chubby
ぽっちゃりした

overweight
体重過多の
obese
肥満の
fat
太った

muscular
筋肉質の

USEFUL SENTENCES

私は中くらいの背丈でちょっとぽっちゃりしています。	I am medium height and a little chubby.
友達の1人は、痩せすぎで悩んでいます。	A friend of mine is worried since she is too skinny.
体重過多が必ずしも悪いこととは限らないでしょ?	Being overweight isn't necessarily a bad thing, is it?
姉は出産してから肥満になりました。	My sister became obese after giving birth.
その年配夫婦は一緒にクルーズ旅行をしています。	The elderly couple is on a cruise together.
この間、彼女がルックスの良い男性と歩いているのを見たわ。	I saw her walking with a good-looking man the other day.

middle-aged 中年の

old 老いた、年を取った
elderly 年配の

good-looking ルックスが良い
handsome (主に男性に)ハンサムな
gorgeous すてきな、魅力的な
attractive 感じの良い
beautiful (主に女性や子どもが)美しい
pretty きれいな、かわいらしい
lovely 愛らしい、魅力的な

体重に関連した表現
- gain weight: 太る
- lose weight: 痩せる
- be on a diet: ダイエット中だ

年代の表現

10代: teens	20代: 20s	30代: 30s

- 初め: one's early ~
  例: **I met her in her early 30s.** 彼女が30代の初めの頃に、私は彼女に会いました。
- 半ば: one's mid-
  例: **He wrote the novel in his mid-20s.** 彼は20代半ばにその小説を書きました。
- 後半: one's late ~
  例: **They are in their late 40s.** 彼らは40代後半です。
- ~と同じ年頃だ: about[around] one's age
  例: **The actress is about my age.** その女優は私と同じ年頃です。

5 顔と頭の形

DL 02_06

顔、肌 have + ~ skin/face

pale skin
青白い肌

fair skin
白い肌

tan skin
日焼けした肌

dark skin
色黒の肌

a round face
丸顔

an oval-shaped face
卵型の顔

a thin〔an oblong〕 face
ほっそりした顔

a square face
四角い顔

pimples
ニキビ、吹き出もの

dark circles
くま

freckles
そばかす、しみ

wrinkles
しわ

acne
ニキビ

dry skin
乾燥肌

mole ほくろ

dimple えくぼ

* **oily skin** 脂性肌

USEFUL SENTENCES

その少女はとても色白でした。	The girl had very fair skin.
卵型の顔ならよかったのに。	I wish I had an oval-shaped face.
赤毛のアンは顔にそばかすがあります。	Anne of Green Gables has freckles on her face.
しわがだんだん増えているのが悩みです。	I'm distressed I'm getting more and more wrinkles.
おへその横にほくろがあります。	I have a mole next to my belly button.
彼はえくぼがすごく魅力的。	He has a very charming dimple.

have + ~ hair

long hair
髪が長い

straight hair
直毛だ

short hair
髪が短い

shoulder-length hair
髪が肩に掛かる

wavy hair
ウェーブが
かかっている

curly hair
巻き毛だ

gray hair
白髪だ

wear a pony tail
ポニーテールにする

have one's hair cut
髪を切る

have one's hair permed
パーマをかける

have one's hair dyed
髪を染める

lose one's hair
髪が抜ける

be bald
はげている

have a beard/a mustache/sideburns
あごひげ／口ひげ／もみ上げがある

USEFUL SENTENCES

私はここ数年、髪を長くしています。	I have had long hair for several years.
その男の子は巻き毛です。	The boy has curly hair.
どれくらいの頻度で髪の毛を切る？	How often do you have your hair cut?
昨日パーマをかけました。	I had my hair permed yesterday.
その男性はもみ上げがありました。	The man had sideburns.

raise one's hand
手を上げる

wave
手を振る

clap one's hands
拍手をする

shake hands with
〜と握手をする

fold one's arms
腕組みをする

carry
持つ、携帯する、運ぶ

pick up
拾い上げる、持ち上げる

touch
触る

USEFUL SENTENCES

質問があれば、手を上げてください。	If you have a question, please raise your hand.
皆さん、拍手してください！	Everybody, clap your hands!
その政治家は、今日500人を超える人たちと握手をしました。	The politician shook hands with over 500 people today.
人を指差すのは失礼です。	Pointing at a person with your finger is rude.
かばんを投げるよ、受け取って！	I'll throw the bag. Catch it!
このドアは引いて開けなきゃ。	You have to pull this door to open it.

point (at)
指し示す

hold
握っている、つかんでいる

hit
打つ、たたく

lift
上に持ち上げる

throw
投げる

catch
(動いている物体を)つかむ、受け取る

pull
引く

push
押す

squeeze
しぼる

twist
ひねる、曲げる

腕を組む
- fold one's arms: 自分の両腕を組むこと
  例：**He talked with his arms folded.** 彼は腕組みしたまま話をしました。
- link arms with ~ / link arms together: 2人が腕組みをすること
  例：**The girls walked along the street with their arms linked.**
  少女たちは腕を組んで道を歩いて行きました。

carry vs. hold
- carry: 持ち歩く、運ぶ、携帯する (移動の意味)
  例：**The man was carrying a briefcase.** その人は書類かばんを持ち歩いていました。
- hold: (手で) 握る／つかむ／持っている (移動の意味×)
  例：**She was holding a teddy bear.** 彼女はくまのぬいぐるみを持っていました。

pick up vs. lift
- pick up: 床面・地表にあるものを拾い上げる
  例：**He picked up a small pebble.** 彼は小石を拾い上げました。
- lift: 上に持ち上げる、位置を引き上げる
  例：**She lifted her face from a book.** 彼女は (読んでいる) 本から顔を上げました。

lie
横たわる

lie on one's face [stomach]
うつ伏せになる

stand up
立ち上がる

fall down
倒れる、転ぶ

bow
おじぎをする

shrug
肩をすくめる

shiver
体を震わせる

hug, embrace
抱く、抱擁する

walk
歩く

USEFUL SENTENCES

そのとき、うつ伏せになって雑誌を読んでいました。	I was lying on my stomach and reading a magazine then.
転ばないように気を付けてください。	Please be careful not to fall down.
彼は肩をすくめて何も言いませんでした。	He shrugged and said nothing.
彼女はよくハグをします。	She often hugs people.
毎日1万歩以上歩きます。	I walk more than 10,000 steps every day.

run
走る、駆ける

jump
ジャンプする

kneel (down)
ひざまずく

kick
足で蹴る

crawl
はう

climb
登る、上る

bend one's knees
かがむ

tiptoe, walk on tiptoe
つま先で静かに歩く

USEFUL SENTENCES

エスカレーターでは走らないでください。	Do not run on escalators.
彼らはひざまずいて祈った。	They knelt down and prayed.
そのボールを私の方へ蹴ってください。	Please kick that ball to me.
その赤ちゃんは最近、よつんばいになってハイハイしています。	The baby crawls on her hands and knees these days.
階段を上るのがつらい。	It's hard for me to climb the stairs.
母が目を覚ますかと思って、そっとつま先歩きしました。	I walked on tiptoe in case my mother woke up.

active
活動的な、積極的な

arrogant
傲慢な、尊大な

bold
大胆な、果敢な

brave
勇敢な

careful
注意深い、気を付ける、
几帳面な

cheerful
はつらつとした、快活な

confident
自信に満ちた

considerate
思慮深い、思いやりのある

curious
好奇心おう盛な

diligent
勤勉な、熱心な

friendly
親切な、優しい、情に厚い

funny
笑える、面白い

USEFUL SENTENCES

ユミは見かけよりも活発です。	Yumi is more active than she looks.
彼はすごく自信にあふれています。	He is very confident in himself.
ケンはとても思慮深いです。	Ken is so considerate.
他人に対し常に寛大であるようにしなさい。	Always try to be generous to others.
衝動的過ぎるのが彼の弱点です。	Being too impulsive is his weakness.
彼はとても謙虚です。	He is very modest.

generous
心の広い、寛大な

gentle
穏やかな、親切な、品のある

honest
正直な、素直な

impulsive
衝動的な

industrious
勤勉な、まめまめしい

jealous
嫉妬している、ねたんでいる

kind
親切な

lazy
怠けた

mature
大人びた

mean
卑劣な、意地悪な

modest
謙虚な、慎重な、質素な

接頭辞を使った反対語

active	↔ inactive	活動していない、活発ではない、消極的な
confident	↔ unconfident	自信のない
considerate	↔ inconsiderate	思慮に欠ける、軽率な
friendly	↔ unfriendly	友好的ではない、不親切な
generous	↔ ungenerous	せせこましい、けちくさい、大らかではない
honest	↔ dishonest	不正直な
kind	↔ unkind	不親切な、薄情な
mature	↔ immature	未熟な、幼稚な

negative 否定的な、悲観的な
obstinate, stubborn 頑固な
open-minded 心の広い、偏見のない
optimistic 楽観的な、楽天的な
outgoing 外向的な、社交的な
passionate 情熱的な
passive 受動的な、消極的な
patient 我慢強い、粘り強い
pessimistic 悲観的な
polite 礼儀正しい、謙遜した
positive 前向きな、好意的な
proud 誇りを持った、自尊心の強い

USEFUL SENTENCES

あんなに頑固な人は見たことがない。	I've never seen anyone so stubborn.
その少年はとても社交的です。	The boy is very outgoing.
とても我慢強いんだね！	You are so patient!
彼女はきちんと道理をわきまえた人です。	She is quite a reasonable person.
タクヤはいつも真面目だ。	Takuya is always serious.
気が小さいのでそんなことはできません。	I am too timid to do such a thing.

reasonable 合理的な、道理をわきまえた
reliable 信頼できる
responsible 責任感のある
rude 無礼な、行儀の悪い
selfish 利己的な
sensitive 繊細な、細かい
serious 深刻な、真面目な
shy 恥ずかしがりの
silly, foolish, stupid 愚かな、ばかげた
thoughtful 思慮深い、配慮のある
timid 気の小さい、勇気のない、臆病な
wise 知恵のある、賢明な、賢い

接頭辞を使った反対語

patient	↔ impatient	せっかちな
polite	↔ impolite	無礼な、行儀の悪い
reasonable	↔ unreasonable	不合理な、理不尽な
reliable	↔ unreliable	信頼できない
responsible	↔ irresponsible	無責任な
selfish	↔ unselfish	利己的ではない、無欲な
thoughtful	↔ unthoughtful	深く考えない、不注意な
wise	↔ unwise	賢明ではない、愚かな

8 感情

DL 02_11

肯定的な感情

delighted とてもうれしい
excited わくわくする、興奮した
grateful, thankful ありがたがった、感謝した
happy 幸せな、気分のいい
interested 関心のある、興味のある
pleased うれしい、満足のいく
proud 自慢に思う、誇らしい
relaxed ゆったりとした、くつろいだ
satisfied 満足な
thrilled とてもわくわくした、興奮した

USEFUL SENTENCES

再会できて本当にうれしいです。	I'm so delighted to meet you again.
彼は遊園地に行くことになってとても喜んでいます。	He is so excited to go to the amusement park.
親切にしてくださってありがとうございます。	I'm grateful that you treated me kindly.
あなたのような友達がいることを誇りに思います。	I'm proud to have a friend like you.
森を散歩すると気分がゆったりします。	Walking through the forest makes me feel relaxed.
自分の人生に満足していますか？	Are you satisfied with your life?

angry 腹を立てた、怒った
annoyed, irritated
イライラした、ムッとした
anxious 不安な、気掛かりな
bored 退屈した
confused 混乱した、混同した
concerned 心配な、気に掛ける
depressed ゆううつな
disappointed 失望した
embarrassed 困惑した、
　　　　　　　　　恥ずかしい思いをした

exhausted 疲れ果てた
frightened おびえた、怖がった
frustrated 挫折した、不満な

furious とても腹を立てた
lonely 寂しい
miserable 悲惨な、不幸な、惨めな
nervous 不安な、焦っている、緊張した
shocked 衝撃を受けた、あぜんとした
stressed ストレスを受けた
tired 疲れた
unhappy 不幸な、不満な
upset 気を悪くした、心の傷ついた
worried 心配した、憂慮する

* **surprised** 驚いた（中立的）

USEFUL SENTENCES

彼女がやたらと干渉し続けるのでイライラする。	I am annoyed that she keeps interfering.
彼の言ったことで混乱する。	I'm confused about what he said.
あなたのせいで恥ずかしい思いをしました。	I was embarrassed because of you.
みんながその若い歌手の突然の死に衝撃を受けました。	Everyone was shocked at the young singer's sudden death.
彼はストレスを受けやすい。	He gets easily stressed.
それについてあまり気に病まないで。	Don't be too upset about it.

3

衣服

_____

Clothing

さまざまな衣類

DL 03_01

 dress shirt
ドレスシャツ、
ワイシャツ

 T-shirt
Tシャツ

 blouse
ブラウス

 sweatshirt
トレーナー

 hoody
パーカー

 sweater
セーター

 cardigan
カーディガン

 vest
ベスト

 jacket
ジャケット

 coat
外套、コート

 suit
スーツ

 dress
ワンピース

 skirt
スカート

 pants
ズボン

USEFUL SENTENCES

ユミはパーカーが好き。	Yumi likes hoodies.
こんな天気の日はカーディガンを持っていかないと。	You'd better pack a cardigan in this weather.
このスカートはどんなトップスともよく合う。	This skirt goes well with any top.
今日、新しいジーンズを買いました。	I bought new jeans today.
彼はめったにネクタイをしません。	He rarely wears a tie.
自分の下着は手洗いしています。	I wash my underwear by hand.

jeans
ジーンズ

shorts
半ズボン

pajamas
寝間着、パジャマ

bathrobe
バスローブ

tie
ネクタイ

socks
靴下

leggings
レギンス

pantyhose
パンティストッキング

stockings
ストッキング

undershirt
肌着

bra
ブラジャー

panties
(女性、子ども用の)
パンティー

underpants
(男性用の)パンツ

boxer shorts
(男性用の)トランクス

* **underwear** 下着

服の詳細なパーツ
collar 襟、カラー
hood (上着などに付いている) フード

sleeve 袖
zipper ファスナー

button ボタン
pocket ポケット

服に関連する動詞表現
• wear: 着ている、着用している (状態)
• put on: 着る、着用する (動作)
• take off: 脱ぐ
• change: 着替える
• fasten: (ファスナー、ボタン、ピンなど) を閉める、止める (↔ unfasten 開ける、外す)

衣類の材質と柄、スタイル

DL 03_02

材質

cotton
綿

silk
シルク、絹織物

wool
羊毛

fur
毛皮

leather
皮革

denim
デニム

linen
リネン、亜麻繊維

nylon
ナイロン

柄、模様

plain
無地の

striped
ストライプの

checked
チェック柄の

polka-dot
水玉模様の

いろいろな柄、模様
- 模様: pattern
- ストライプ柄: stripes
- 水玉模様: polka dots
- 花柄: floral[flower] pattern
- アーガイル柄（ダイヤモンド柄）: argyle pattern

formal 正装の
neat, tidy 端正な、こぎれいな

untidy
きちんと
していない

informal, casual
普段着の、カジュアルな

**fashionable,
stylish, trendy**
流行を追った、
おしゃれな

loose
ゆったりとした

tight
ぴったりとした、
きつい

USEFUL SENTENCES

綿の服しか着られません。	I can only wear cotton clothes.
ストライプシャツを着た、あそこの男性を見て。	Look at that guy wearing a striped shirt over there.
水玉模様のワンピース、よく似合うね。	A polka-dot dress looks good on you.
その日はカジュアルな服でいいよ。	You can wear casual clothes that day.
あの男の人、すごくおしゃれ。	That man is very fashionable.
このTシャツ、きつすぎ。	This T-shirt is too tight.

雑貨、アクセサリー

`DL 03_03`

hat
帽子

cap
つばの付いた帽子

gloves
手袋

handkerchief
ハンカチ

glasses, spectacles
眼鏡

sunglasses
サングラス

belt
ベルト

watch
腕時計

scarf
スカーフ、マフラー

shawl
ショール

USEFUL SENTENCES

日差しが強いから帽子をかぶらないと。	The sun is so strong that you have to wear a hat.
手がとても冷たいから、手袋をしないと。	My hands are so cold that I have to wear gloves.
ベルトをしなかったから、やたらとズボンが落ちてくる。	My pants keep falling down because I didn't put on a belt.
スマートフォンがあるから、腕時計をしている人が近頃あまりいません。	These days not many people wear watches since they have smartphones.
こんな天気だからマフラーをしよう。	I'll wear a scarf in this weather.
私はたいていエコバッグを持ち歩いています。	I usually carry a reusable shopping bag.
梅雨の時期にはいつも傘を持ち歩いています。	I always carry an umbrella with me during the rainy season.

suitcase
旅行かばん

briefcase
書類かばん

backpack
リュック

shoulder bag
ショルダーバッグ

handbag
ハンドバッグ

reusable shopping bag
エコバッグ

purse, wallet
財布

umbrella
傘

parasol
日傘

wear ~
- a hat, a cap: 帽子をかぶる
- a scarf/a muffler/a shawl: スカーフ／マフラー／ショールを巻く
- gloves: 手袋をはめる
- a belt: ベルトをする
- glasses/sunglasses: 眼鏡／サングラスをかける
- a watch: 腕時計を着ける
- a hairpin/a hair tie/a necklace/a bracelet/earrings/a ring/a brooch:
  ヘアピン／ヘアゴム／ネックレス／ブレスレット／イヤリング／指輪／ブローチを着ける

傘を差す、たたむ
- put up[hold] an umbrella: 傘を差す
- close[fold] an umbrella: 傘をたたむ
- open an umbrella: 傘を開く

purse vs. wallet
purseとwalletはどちらも日本語では「財布」ですが、一般的にはwalletが、紙幣やコイン、カード、名刺などを入れる財布を指します。purseはwalletと同じ意味で使われることもありますが、ハンドバッグを指す場合もあります。

jewelry
宝石類、アクセサリー

necklace
ネックレス

bracelet
ブレスレット

earrings
イヤリング

ring
指輪

brooch
ブローチ

hair tie
ヘアゴム

headband
ヘアバンド、カチューシャ

hair pin
ヘアピン

USEFUL SENTENCES

その中年女性は、アクセサリーを
たくさん身に着けていました。

妹に銀のネックレスを買いました。

小さなイヤリングを着けるのが好き。

見たことない指輪をしてるね。

母がこのブローチを私にくれたの。

ヘアゴムで髪を結びなよ。

The middle-aged woman wore lots of jewelry.

I bought a silver necklace for my sister.

I prefer to wear small earrings.

You're wearing a ring I haven't seen before.

My mother gave me this brooch.

Tie your hair with a hair tie.

sneakers
スニーカー

running shoes
運動靴、ランニングシューズ

high heels
ハイヒール

flats, flat shoes
フラットシューズ

wedge heels
ウェッジソール

loafers
ローファー

sandals
サンダル

boots
ブーツ、長靴
(**rain boots** レインブーツ)

flip-flops
ビーチサンダル

slippers
スリッパ、室内履き

USEFUL SENTENCES

ジーンズにスニーカーがいちばん楽。	Wearing jeans and sneakers is the most comfortable.
ハイヒールは一度も履いたことがありません。	I have never worn high heels.
子どもの頃は雨の日に長靴を履いていました。	I wore rain boots on rainy days when I was a child.
室内履きで外に出ちゃダメ。	Don't go outside in your slippers.

靴のいろいろなパーツ
- heel: かかと
- insole: 中敷き
- outsole: 外底
- bottom of a shoe: 靴の底
- shoelace: 靴ひも

CHAPTER

食生活

Food

食材（1）―穀物と野菜

DL 04_01

穀物

rice 米
brown rice 玄米
wheat 小麦
barley 大麦
beans 豆
soybeans 大豆
black beans 黒豆
kidney beans インゲン豆
peas エンドウ豆
red beans 小豆
corn トウモロコシ
rye ライ麦
oats オート麦
flour 小麦粉
whole wheat 全粒粉

USEFUL SENTENCES

玄米と全粒粉は健康にいい。	Brown rice and whole wheat are good for your health.
キャベツは胃にいいんだって。	They say cabbage is good for your stomach.
カレーには、ジャガイモとニンジン、玉ネギ、豚肉を入れます。	I put potatoes, carrots, onions and pork in my curry.
息子はピーマンを食べません。	My son doesn't eat bell peppers.
ニンニクを入れないとシチューがおいしくありません。	If you don't put garlic in it, the stew doesn't taste good.

Chinese cabbage
白菜

white radish
大根

cabbage
キャベツ

lettuce
レタス

zucchini
ズッキーニ

pumpkin
カボチャ

cucumber
キュウリ

egg plant
ナス

carrot
ニンジン、赤大根

potato
ジャガイモ

sweet potato
サツマイモ

green onion, scallion
ネギ

onion
玉ネギ

leek
ニラ

hot pepper
唐辛子

bell pepper, sweet pepper
ピーマン

garlic
ニンニク

ginger
生姜

mushroom
キノコ

bean sprout
モヤシ

spinach
ホウレン草

perilla leaf
エゴマの葉

lotus root
レンコン

79

2 食材 (2)—海産物、肉類、卵

DL 04_02

海産物 **seafood** 海産物

pollack
スケトウダラ

mackerel
サバ

cod
タラ

anchovy
カタクチイワシ

halibut
カレイ

trout
マス

tuna
マグロ

salmon
サケ

hairtail, cutlassfish
タチウオ

Pacific saury
サンマ

sardine
イワシ

seaweed
海藻類

USEFUL SENTENCES

海産物の中でエビがいちばん好き。	I like shrimp the most among seafood.
サバやサンマのような青魚が体にいいんだって。	They say blue-backed fish like mackerel and Pacific saury are good for your health.
海藻類は血液をきれいにするのに役立ちます。	Seaweed helps make our blood clear.
彼はカキアレルギーです。	He's allergic to oysters.
牛肉より豚肉の方が好きです。	I like pork better than beef.
卵の黄身はコレステロールを多く含んでいます。	Egg yolks contain a lot of cholesterol.

squid
イカ

octopus
タコ

oyster
カキ

clam
二枚貝

mussel
イガイ

shrimp
エビ

crab
カニ

lobster
ロブスター

肉類、卵

meat
肉

beef
牛肉

pork
豚肉

lamb
子羊の肉

chicken
鶏肉

duck meat
カモ肉

egg
卵

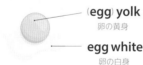
(egg) yolk
卵の黄身

egg white
卵の白身

魚の分類
- bluefish: 青魚
- whitefish: 白身魚
- saltwater fish: 海水魚
- freshwater fish: 淡水魚

鶏肉のさまざまな部位

breast むね肉	leg もも肉 (= drumstick)	wing 手羽

牛肉、豚肉のさまざまな部位

sirloin サーロイン	tenderloin テンダーロイン	pork belly 豚バラ肉
beef rib 牛カルビ	pork rib 豚のあばら肉	

`DL 04_03`

果物 **fruits** 果物

apple
リンゴ

pear
梨

orange
オレンジ

strawberry
イチゴ

grapes
ブドウ

peach
桃

watermelon
スイカ

mandarin
マンダリンオレンジ

persimmon
柿

apricot
アンズ

plum
スモモ

grapefruit
グレープフルーツ

USEFUL SENTENCES

朝に食べるリンゴは健康にとてもいい。
The apple we eat in the morning is very good for our health.

犬はブドウを食べない方がいい。
Dogs shouldn't eat grapes.

一番好きな果物？ 桃。
My favorite fruit? Peaches.

干し柿は家で作れるよ。
You can make dried persimmons at home.

オレンジとグレープフルーツは見た目が似ています。
Oranges and grapefruits look alike.

banana
バナナ

mango
マンゴー

pineapple
パイナップル

kiwi fruit
キウイ

pomegranate
ザクロ

fig
イチジク

jujube
ナツメ

raisin
干しブドウ

ナッツ類   **nuts** ナッツ類

peanuts
ピーナッツ

chestnuts
栗

almonds
アーモンド

walnuts
クルミ

pine nuts
松の実

USEFUL SENTENCES

ナッツ類を毎日食べるのは健康にいい。

ピーナッツって豆？

Eating nuts every day is good for your health.

Are peanuts beans?

果物に関連する表現
- 果物を摘む: pick ~
- 果物をむく: peel ~
- 果汁をしぼる: make juice out of ~
- 果肉: flesh
- 皮: peel
- 果汁: juice

食材 (4)—乳製品、薬味

DL 04_04

乳製品 **dairy〔milk〕products** 乳製品

milk
牛乳
low fat milk
低脂肪乳

yogurt
ヨーグルト
fat-free yogurt
無脂肪ヨーグルト

cheese **butter** **soybean milk**
チーズ バター 豆乳

USEFUL SENTENCES

牛乳はカルシウムの主要な供給源です。	Milk is a great source of calcium.
牛乳を消化できません。	I can't digest milk.
彼女は家でヨーグルトを作っています。	She makes yogurt at home.
母は家でみそを作っています。	My mom makes soybean paste at home.
オリーブオイルは体にいい。	Olive oil is good for our health.
酢とからしを取ってください。	Pass me the vinegar and the mustard, please.

seasonings, condiments 薬味、調味料

salt 塩

sugar 砂糖

pepper こしょう

red pepper powder 唐辛子粉

soy sauce しょうゆ

soybean paste みそ

red pepper paste 唐辛子みそ

sesame salt ごま塩

cooking oil 食用油

olive oil オリーブオイル

sesame oil ごま油

perilla oil えごま油

sesame ごま

vinegar 酢

mustard からし

Japanese horseraddish, wasabi わさび

dressing ドレッシング

marinade (肉などを漬け込む)たれ

cut
切る

chop
切り刻む、みじん切りする

slice
薄く切る、薄切りにする

dice, cube
角切りにする

julienne
千切りにする

peel
皮をむく

grate
すりおろす

mince
肉をミンチにする

mash
すりつぶす

mix 混ぜ合わせる
stir かき混ぜる、かき回す

whisk
泡立てる

USEFUL SENTENCES

玉ネギを薄切りにしてオリーブオイルで炒めて。	Slice the onions thinly and stir-fry them in olive oil.
大根を角切りにしました。	I diced a white radish.
キャベツを千切りにしてください。	Julienne the cabbage, please.
ジャガイモの皮をむいていて手を切った。	I cut my finger while peeling the potatoes.
生姜をすりおろしてください。	Please grate some ginger.
彼はティースプーンでコーヒーをかき混ぜた。	He stirred his coffee with a teaspoon.

pour
注ぐ

blanch
ゆがく

boil
沸かす、ゆでる

steam
蒸す

stir-fry
炒める

deep-fry
たっぷりの油で揚げる

grill
網焼きにする

barbecue
炭火で焼く

roast オーブンや火で焼く
bake パン・お菓子を焼く

USEFUL SENTENCES

ホウレン草をさっとゆがいて。	Blanch the spinach a little.
トウモロコシをゆでて食べます。	I'm going to boil the corn and eat it.
用意した野菜を中火で炒めてください。	Stir-fry prepared vegetables over medium heat.
魚は網焼きにすると一番おいしい。	Fish tastes best when you grill it.
家で初めてマドレーヌを焼いてみました。	It's my first time baking madeleines at home.

6 キッチン用品、容器

DL 04_06

saucepan
片手鍋

frying pan
フライパン

wok
中華鍋

pot
鍋、深鍋

colander
水切りボウル、ざる

bowl
ボウル、おわん

plate
皿

tray
お盆

jar
ジャムなどを
入れておく瓶

cutting board
まな板

kitchen knife
包丁

scissors
はさみ

peeler
ピーラー

spatula, fish slice
フライ返し

ladle
お玉

rice paddle
しゃもじ

USEFUL SENTENCES

各種あるまな板の中でも、木のものが一番です。	Of the various cutting boards, a wooden one is best.
包丁はどこで研げる？	Where can I sharpen my kitchen knife?
はさみは台所で使い道が多い。	Scissors are useful in the kitchen.
ピーラーでじゃがいもの皮をむきました。	I peeled the potatoes with a peeler.
目玉焼きを作る時、フライ返しが必要？	Do you need a spatula when you fry eggs?
そのしゃもじでご飯をよそって。	Scoop the rice with that rice paddle.

whisk
泡立て器

(kitchen) scales
クッキングスケール

can opener
缶切り

bottle opener
栓抜き

spoon
スプーン

chopsticks
箸

kettle
やかん

teacup
ティーカップ

glass
グラス

mug
マグカップ

apron
エプロン

dishwashing liquid(detergent)
食器用洗剤

sponge
(食器洗い用の)スポンジ

dishcloth, dishtowel, dishrag
布巾

USEFUL SENTENCES

台所にクッキングスケールがあると役に立ちます。 Scales in the kitchen are useful.

栓抜き取ってくれますか？ Could you give me the bottle opener?

彼は箸の使い方が上手ではありません。 He's not very good at using chopsticks.

エプロンを着けて仕事しなさい。そうしないと 服が汚れるよ。 Work with an apron on. Otherwise, your clothes will get dirty.

母は天然食器用洗剤を使っています。 My mother uses natural dishwashing liquid.

こまめに布巾を消毒しています。 I often disinfect the dishtowel.

UNIT 7 味

DL 04_07

動詞

dine 食事する
taste 味見する
chew かむ、かみくだく
swallow 飲み込む
bite かむ、かみつく
sip すする、少しずつ飲む
gulp ごくごく飲む

形容詞

delicious, tasty, yummy, savory おいしい、味のよい
sweet 甘い
salty しょっぱい、塩辛い
hot 辛い
sour 酸っぱい

USEFUL SENTENCES

薄味過ぎないか味見してみて。	Taste it to see if it is bland.
食べ物は十分にかんだ方がいい。	Make sure you chew your food enough.
今日は塩辛い物をたくさん食べました。	I ate a lot of salty food today.
香辛料の効いた辛い食べ物は問題ありません。	I have no problem with hot and spicy food.
妊娠すると酸っぱい物が食べたくなりますか？	Do you want to eat sour food when you're pregnant?

sweet-and-sour 甘酸っぱい	**bitter** 苦い
spicy 香辛料の効いた	**bland** 薄味の、あっさりした
oily, greasy 脂っこい、くどい	**fishy** 生臭い
crunchy, crispy サクサクした	**chewy** 歯応えのある
mild 辛みや苦みの少ない、 まろやかな	**strong** 香りの強い、(飲料が)濃い
iced 氷を入れた	**sparkling, carbonated** 炭酸の入った

USEFUL SENTENCES

甘酸っぱい物が食べたいです。　　　　　　　I'd like to eat sweet-and-sour food.

この食べ物、苦い味がしない？　　　　　　　This food tastes bitter, doesn't it?

生臭い食べ物が苦手です。　　　　　　　　　I find it hard to eat fishy food.

この揚げ野菜はすごくサクサクしている。　These fried vegetables are so crispy.

アイスティーを１杯お願い。　　　　　　　　Give me a cup of iced tea.

8 外食

DL 04_08

make a reservation 予約する

order 注文する

pay the check 会計する

go Dutch 割り勘にする

dine together 一緒に食事する、会食する

treat おごる

treat someone to lunch/dinner 昼食を／夕食をおごる

takeout (food) 持ち帰り用の食べ物

~ to go ～ (食べ物) を持って帰る

USEFUL SENTENCES

中華料理店に予約を入れました。	I made a reservation at a Chinese restaurant.
今、注文してもいいですか？	May I order now?
あの日は割り勘にしました。	We went Dutch that day.
今週の木曜日、うちのチームの会食があります。	Our team will dine together this Thursday.
今夜は私が夕食をおごります。	I'll treat you to dinner tonight.
チーズピザのラージサイズ1つ、持ち帰りでお願いします。	One large cheese pizza to go, please.

cafe
カフェ

restaurant
レストラン

bar
バー

fast food restaurant
ファストフード店

buffet
ビュッフェ

cafeteria
カフェテリア（セルフサービスの飲食店）、
社内食堂、学食

food stall 食べ物の露店、屋台
food truck キッチンカー
full course meal コース料理
appetizer アペタイザー、前菜
main course, entree メイン料理
dessert デザート
today's special 今日の特別料理
chef's special 料理長のスペシャル［お薦め］料理

USEFUL SENTENCES

今日はファストフード店で昼食を取りました。	I had lunch at a fast food restaurant today.
ビュッフェに行くといつも食べ過ぎてしまう。	I always overeat at the buffet.
その祭りには屋台がたくさん出ます。	There are many food stalls at the festival.
キッチンカーを見たことないの？	Haven't you ever seen a food truck?
今日のメイン料理は何ですか？	What's the main course of the day?
料理長のお薦め料理にしよう。	Let's have the chef's special.

5

住居

Housing

1 住居全般

build a house
家を建てる

**go house-
hunting**
家探しをする

**lease(rent)
a house**
家を借りる

**buy(purchase)
a house**
家を買う

move
引っ越す

move in/out
引っ越してくる／引っ越していく

get(take out) a loan
ローンを組む

**get(take out)
a mortgage (loan)**
不動産担保ローンを組む

real estate agency
不動産業者

real estate agent
不動産業者

USEFUL SENTENCES

最近、週末のたびに家探しをしています。	These days, I go house-hunting every weekend.
彼女は銀行でローンを組んで家を買いました。	She took out a loan from a bank and bought a house.
その不動産業者が家をいくつか薦めてくれました。	The real estate agent recommended me several houses.
彼はワンルームマンションに住んでいます。	He lives in a studio.
入居者が何カ月も毎月の家賃を払ってないんだって？	Your tenant hasn't paid the monthly rent for months?

townhouse
タウンハウス

mansion
大邸宅

**condominium,
condo**
(分譲)マンション

**apartment
building**
アパート、(賃貸)マンション

studio ワンルームマンション
furnished 家具が備え付けられた (‥ **unfurnished**)
rented house 借家
deposit 保証金、敷金
(monthly) rent 家賃、部屋代
landlord, landlady, owner 家主
tenant, renter 入居者

家の外部、内部

DL 05_02

家の外部

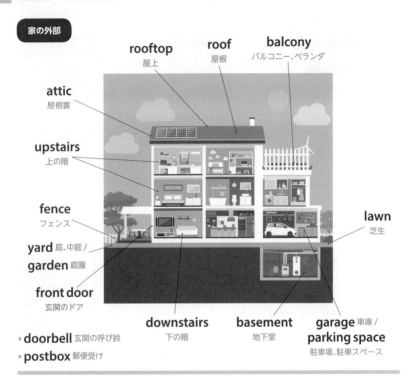

rooftop
屋上

roof
屋根

balcony
バルコニー、ベランダ

attic
屋根裏

upstairs
上の階

fence
フェンス

lawn
芝生

yard 庭、中庭 /
garden 庭園

front door
玄関のドア

* doorbell 玄関の呼び鈴

* postbox 郵便受け

downstairs
下の階

basement
地下室

garage 車庫 /
parking space
駐車場、駐車スペース

USEFUL SENTENCES

屋上で植物をたくさん育てています。	We grow a lot of plants on our rooftop.
バルコニーがない家は検討しません。	I wouldn't consider a house without a balcony.
私の部屋は上の階にあります。	My room is upstairs.
庭園のある家に住むのが母の夢だ。	My mom's dream is to live in a house with a garden.
その家は駐車スペースがある。	The house has a parking space.
地下室にいろいろな物を保管しています。	I keep a lot of things in the basement.

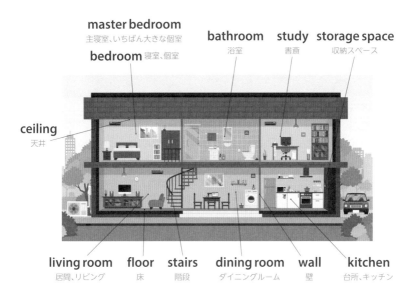

master bedroom
主寝室、いちばん大きな個室

bedroom 寝室、個室

bathroom
浴室

study
書斎

storage space
収納スペース

ceiling
天井

living room
居間、リビング

floor
床

stairs
階段

dining room
ダイニングルーム

wall
壁

kitchen
台所、キッチン

USEFUL SENTENCES

その家はいくつ個室がありますか？	How many bedrooms does the house have?
うちの浴室には浴槽がありません。	We don't have a bathtub in our bathroom.
天井に星型のステッカーをたくさん貼りました。	I put a lot of star-shaped stickers on the ceiling.
彼らは毎晩リビングに集まって一緒にテレビを見ます。	They get together in the living room and watch TV every evening.
台所に冷蔵庫が2台あります。	There are two refrigerators in the kitchen.
毎日床をモップがけします。	I mop the floor every day.

3 家具、家電製品

DL 05_03

家具

wardrobe
衣装ダンス

built-in wardrobe, closet
作り付けの衣装ダンス、クローゼット

dresser, chest of drawers
整理ダンス

dressing table
化粧台、ドレッサー

bed
ベッド

bedside table
ベッドサイドテーブル

couch, sofa
ソファー

bookcase, bookshelf
本棚

(dining) table
食卓

shoe closet, shoe shelf
靴箱

＊浴室の設備

toilet 便器
bathtub 浴槽
shower シャワー
wash basin, sink
洗面台

USEFUL SENTENCES

新しいアパートには作り付けの衣装ダンスがあります。	The new apartment has a built-in wardrobe.
整理ダンスをもう1つ買う必要があります。	I need to buy another chest of drawers.
このソファー、本当に心地いい！	This sofa is really comfortable!
本棚が3つあるのに、本を入れるのに足りない。	There are three bookcases, but they're not enough for my books.
靴箱、自分で作ったの？	Did you make your own shoe closet?
うちの浴室には小さな浴槽があります。	There's a small bathtub in my bathroom.

dresser vs. chest of drawers
どちらも引き出しのある「整理ダンス」を指しますが、dresserは通常、引き出しの上に鏡のある構造です。drawerは「引き出し1つ」を指し、chest of drawersで「整理ダンス」になります。

light
照明、電灯

television
テレビ

vacuum cleaner 電気掃除機
robot vacuum cleaner
ロボット掃除機

air conditioner
エアコン

electric fan
扇風機

desktop computer
デスクトップパソコン

laptop (computer)
ノート型パソコン

washing machine
洗濯機

dryer
(衣類)乾燥機

USEFUL SENTENCES

明かりをつけて本を読んだら？	Why don't you turn on the light and read a book?
最近のエアコンは以前ほど電気を使いません。	Today's air conditioners don't use as much electricity as they used to.
このノート型パソコンは5年前のものになります。	This laptop is five years old.
家事の時間を最も削減したのは洗濯機です。	It's the washing machine that cut the housework time the most.

top-loading vs. front-loading
洗濯機には「縦型洗濯機」と「ドラム式洗濯機」があります。英語ではこの2つをどのように表現するでしょうか？ 「縦型洗濯機」は洗濯物を上から入れます。ですから、top-loading washing machine と言います。一方、「ドラム式洗濯機」は洗濯物を前から入れます。ですから、front-loading washing machineと言います。面白いネーミングですね。

iron
アイロン

outlet
プラグの差込口、コンセント

sewing machine
ミシン

hair dryer
ヘアドライヤー

remote control
リモコン

electric razor
電気かみそり

humidifier
加湿器

dehumidifier
除湿器

air cleaner, air purifier
空気清浄機

radiator
ラジエーター、放熱器

USEFUL SENTENCES

冬はとても乾燥するので加湿器をつけないといけません。

It's so dry in winter that I have to turn on the humidifier.

最近は空気清浄機のある家が多い。

These days, many houses have an air cleaner.

turn on/off ~ つける／消す
家電製品（の電源）を「入れる」「つける」は turn on ~.「止める」「消す」は turn off ~ と表現します。

例：**Let's turn on the air conditioner. It's so hot in here.**
エアコンを入れよう。ここは暑すぎる。

例：**I think you can turn off the air purifier now.**
もう空気清浄機は止めてもよさそうです。

kitchen cabinets
台所の食器棚

sink シンク

refrigerator
冷蔵庫

freezer 冷凍庫

kitchen stove, gas stove
ガスレンジ

induction stove, induction cooktop
IHレンジ

oven
オーブン

kitchen hood, range hood
レンジフード

microwave
電子レンジ

electric rice cooker
電気炊飯器

dishwasher
食器洗い機

toaster
トースター

coffee maker
コーヒーメーカー

blender
ミキサー

electric kettle
電気湯沸かし器

water purifier
浄水器

trash can
ごみ箱

USEFUL SENTENCES

最近、わが家にIHレンジを設置しました。 | I recently installed an induction stove in my house.

日本でも食器洗い機を使う家庭が増えています。 | More and more homes are using dishwashers in Japan.

友達が誕生日プレゼントにコーヒーメーカーをくれました。 | A friend of mine gave me a coffee maker for my birthday.

インテリア、家の修繕、掃除

DL 05_05

renovate[remodel] the house
家をリフォームする

repair the house
家を修理する（壊れたところを修理する）

paint the house/a room
家／部屋を塗装する

unblock[clear, unclog] the drain[sewer]
排水口の詰まりを解消する

change a light bulb
電球を取り替える

decorate[redecorate] the interior of ～のインテリアを飾る（新しくする）
repaper the walls 壁紙を張り替える
redo the floors 床を張り替える
repaint the cabinets 戸棚を塗り直す
unclog the toilet 便器の詰まりを解消する

USEFUL SENTENCES

家のリフォームに2カ月かかりました。	It took us two months to renovate the house.
配管工を呼んで排水口の詰まりを解消しました。	I called a plumber and had him unblock the drain.
電球を自分で取り替えることもできないの？	Can't you change a light bulb yourself?
家のインテリアにお金をたくさんかけました。	I spent a lot of money decorating the interior of my house.
引っ越し先の家は壁紙を張り替えをすればいいだけです。	All you have to do for the house when you move in is to repaper the walls.
床を張り替えないといけないと思います。	I think we need to redo the floor.

vacuum cleaner
電気掃除機

cleanser
(清掃用)洗剤

mop
モップ

rag
雑巾

broom
ほうき

dustpan
ちりとり

garbage bag
ごみ袋

trash can
ごみ箱

washing machine
洗濯機

dryer
(衣類)乾燥機

laundry basket
洗濯かご

laundry detergent
洗濯せっけん

fabric[fiber] softener
柔軟剤

clothespin
洗濯バサミ

drying rack
物干し台

USEFUL SENTENCES

電気掃除機が壊れました。	The vacuum cleaner is broken.
モップで床をよく拭かないと。	You should wipe the floor well with a mop.
雑巾で窓枠を拭いて。	Wipe the windowsill with a rag.
指定のごみ袋を使わなければなりません。	You must use a designated plastic garbage bag.
柔軟剤を使わないといけませんか？	Do I have to use fabric softener?
物干し台に洗濯物を干します。	I hang clothes on a drying rack.

人間関係

Relationship

さまざまな人間関係

DL 06_01

家系図
family tree

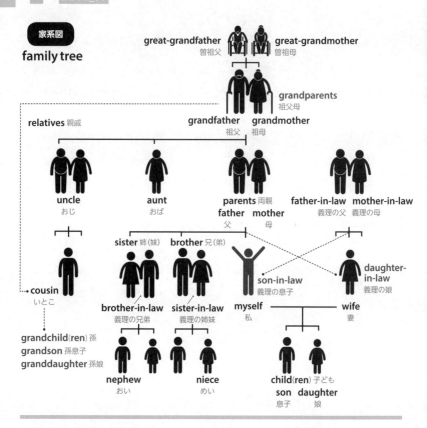

great-grandfather 曽祖父		great-grandmother 曽祖母	
	grandparents 祖父母		
grandfather 祖父	grandmother 祖母		

relatives 親戚

uncle おじ
aunt おば
parents 両親 / father 父 / mother 母
father-in-law 義理の父
mother-in-law 義理の母

cousin いとこ

grandchild(ren) 孫
grandson 孫息子
granddaughter 孫娘

sister 姉(妹)
brother 兄(弟)
son-in-law 義理の息子
daughter-in-law 義理の娘

brother-in-law 義理の兄弟
sister-in-law 義理の姉妹
myself 私
wife 妻

nephew おい
niece めい
child(ren) 子ども / son 息子 / daughter 娘

USEFUL SENTENCES

義理の母は90代ですがとても元気です。	My mother-in-law is in her 90s, but she is very healthy.
めいは大学生です。	My niece is a college student.
彼は継父ですが実の父のようにいい人です。	He is my stepfather, but he is as good as a real father.
彼女は私の同僚です。	She is my coworker.
彼と私はただの学友です。	He and I are just schoolmates.

stepmother
継母、義母

stepsister
異父姉(妹)、異母(姉妹)

stepfather
継父、義父

stepbrother
異父兄(弟)、異母(兄弟)

single parent シングルペアレント
(**single father** シングルファーザー, **single mother** シングルマザー)

* **sibling** 兄弟姉妹
* **twins** 双子
* **triplets** 三つ子

---

friend, buddy 友達
acquaintance 知り合い、知人
colleague, coworker 同僚
schoolmate 同じ学校の友達、学友
classmate 同じクラスの友達、級友
roommate ルームメイト
partner パートナー、配偶者、共同経営者

---

in-laws
in-lawは「姻戚」、つまり結婚によって結ばれた親戚を指します。結婚して法的に親戚になるため、in-lawと呼ぶのですね。

colleague vs. coworker
colleagueとcoworkerはどちらも「同僚」と翻訳できます。しかし、2つの単語には違いがあります。colleagueは同じ職種、特に同じ専門職に就いている人を指し、coworkerは同じ会社で働く職位が同じくらいの人を指します。

2 交際、関係

DL 06_02

introduce 〜を紹介する

get to know 〜と知り合う

get acquainted with 〜と面識を持つ、親しくなる

make friends with, get to be friends with 〜と親しくなる

get along with, get on well with, be on good terms with
〜と仲良くする、仲が良い

hang out with 〜と一緒に過ごす

be sociable, be outgoing 社交的だ

be shy, be shy of strangers 人見知りをする

visit, call on 〜を訪ねる

have good manners 礼儀正しい

have no manners 礼儀知らずだ、無礼だ

USEFUL SENTENCES

彼とはロンドンで知り合いました。	I got to know him in London.
彼らは中学校のとき親しくなりました。	They made friends with each other when they were in middle school.
ミカはみんなと仲がいい。	Mika gets along well with people.
ユウスケはとても社交的です。	Yusuke is very sociable.
人見知りなんです。	I'm shy of strangers.
彼は本当に礼儀知らずだ。	He really has no manners.

fall out with ～と仲が悪くなる、仲違いする

talk about someone behind one's back ～の陰で悪口を言う

argue with, have an argument with ～と口げんかする

quarrel with ～と争う、けんかする

fight with ～と殴り合いのけんかをする

---

make up with, reconcile with ～と仲直りする

USEFUL SENTENCES

彼と仲違いしたの？

Did you fall out with him?

人と口げんかをするのは嫌いです。

I don't like to argue with people.

argue, quarrel, fight
argue, quarrel, fight は、いずれも「争う」という意味を持っています。しかし、3つの単語には違い
があります。
・argue:「論戦する」「言い争いをする」という意味で、けんかとまではいかなくても、言葉で何かに
　　　　ついて議論を戦わせるときに使います。
・quarrel: argue よりも激しい感情で言い争うことを指します。実際に口げんかをすることを指します。
・fight: 身体的暴力をふるってまで争うことを指します。

結婚、別れ、死別

DL 06_03

have[go on] a blind date ブラインドデートをする
have a crush on ～に熱を上げる
fall in love with ～と恋に落ちる
fall in love at first sight with ～に一目ぼれする
ask someone out (on a date) ～にデートを申し込む
have a date with ～と（1回）デートする
be in a relationship 付き合う、交際する
be in a romantic relationship with ～と付き合う、交際する
break up with (交際していた関係で) ～と別れる

USEFUL SENTENCES

彼は毎週末ブラインドデートをします。	He has a blind date every weekend.
シンディーは彼に熱を上げているに違いありません。	Cindy must have a crush on the man.
2人は一目で恋に落ちました。	The two fell in love at first sight.
彼女にデートを申し込んだ？	Did you ask her out?

propose to
～にプロポーズする

get engaged to
～と婚約する

bride
新婦

get married to
～と結婚する

groom, bridegroom
新郎

engagement 婚約

fiance (女性から見た男性の) 婚約者 / **fiancee** (男性から見た女性の) 婚約者

wedding 結婚式

love marriage 恋愛結婚

arranged marriage 見合い結婚

matchmaker 仲人

be married 既婚だ

USEFUL SENTENCES

彼氏にプロポーズしました。

I proposed to my boyfriend.

新郎がとても緊張しています。

The groom is very nervous.

彼は私の婚約者です。

He is my fiance.

結婚式は省きたいです。

I'd like to skip the wedding.

恋愛結婚でしたか？　お見合い結婚でしたか？

Did you have a love marriage or an arranged marriage?

DL 06_04

hold a wedding reception
結婚披露宴を開く

go on one's honeymoon
新婚旅行に行く
go to ~ for one's honeymoon
新婚旅行で~に行く

have an affair with
~と浮気する
cheat on
~をだまして浮気する

get divorced
離婚する
divorce 離婚

---

lose one's wife/husband, be widowed 妻／夫を亡くす
widow 夫を亡くした女性
widower 妻を亡くした男性

---

be single, be unmarried, be not married 独身[未婚]だ
live on one's own 独身[未婚]で過ごす
remain on one's own 独身[未婚]を維持する

USEFUL SENTENCES

新婚旅行は南フランスへ行きたいです。	I'd like to go to southern France for my honeymoon.
その男が浮気したって？	Did the man cheat on her?
その女優がまた離婚しました。	The actress got divorced again.
彼女は5年前に事故で夫を亡くしました。	She lost her husband in an accident five years ago.
独身です。	I am single.
一生独身で暮らすつもり？	Are you going to live on your own for the rest of your life?

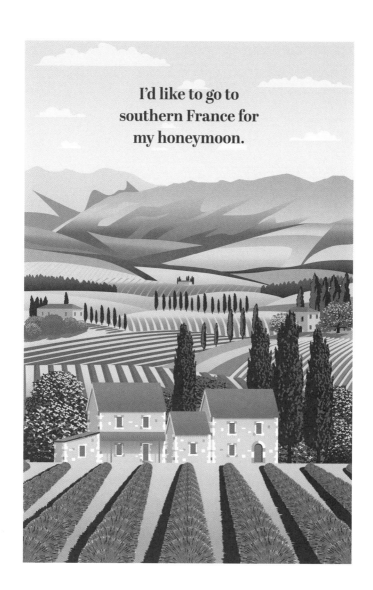

I'd like to go to
southern France for
my honeymoon.

CHAPTER

7

健康

Health

生理現象

DL 07_01

 pulse
脈拍、脈打つ

 **heart beat** 心臓の鼓動
heart rate 心拍数

 **breathe**
息をする、呼吸する
breath 呼吸

 **shiver**
震える

 **sweat**
汗、汗をかく

 bleed
血が出る
blood 血

 blood pressure
血圧

 **blood sugar**
血糖

USEFUL SENTENCES

医者が患者の脈を測った。 — The doctor measured the patient's pulse.

彼の心拍数は1分間に50回足らずです。 — His heart rate is less than 50 beats per minute.

細かいほこりのせいで呼吸するのがつらかった。 — It was hard to breathe because of the fine dust.

その男性は熱い食べ物を食べると、たくさん 汗をかきます。 — The man sweats a lot when he eats hot food.

正常な血圧はいくつですか？ — What's the normal blood pressure?

digest 消化する (**digestion** 消化)

absorb 吸収する (**absorption** 吸収)

secrete 分泌する (**secretion** 分泌物)

go to the bathroom〔toilet〕, relieve oneself
用を足す、大便・小便をする

pee, take a pee
小便をする

urine, pee 小便、おしっこ

**move one's bowels,
poop, defecate**
大便をする

poop, feces, excrement 大便、うんち

fart, break wind
おならをする

hold in (a) fart
おならを我慢する

burp
げっぷをする

hold in a burp
げっぷを我慢する

vomit, throw up
吐く

USEFUL SENTENCES

胃や腸などの器官が消化を担っています。
The stomach, intestines and other organs are responsible for digestion.

トイレに行こうと急いでいます。
I'm in a hurry to go to the bathroom.

外で大便をすることができません。
I can't poop outside my house.

人前ではげっぷを我慢すべきだよ。
You have to hold in a burp in front of people.

2 栄養、食習慣

DL 07_02

nutrition
栄養、栄養摂取

carbohydrate
炭水化物

protein
タンパク質

fat
脂肪

saturated fat
飽和脂肪

unsaturated fat
不飽和脂肪

dietary fiber
食物繊維

cholesterol
コレステロール

vitamin ビタミン
mineral ミネラル
iron 鉄分
sugar 糖、砂糖
nutritious 栄養価の高い
nutrient 栄養素、栄養分
essential nutrient 必須栄養素

USEFUL SENTENCES

炭水化物の食べ過ぎだ。少し減らさなきゃ。

I eat too many carbohydrates. I need to cut down on them a little.

動物性タンパク質と植物性タンパク質があります。

There is animal protein and vegetable protein.

飽和脂肪は体によくないから食べ過ぎるべきではありません。

Saturated fat is bad for your body, so you shouldn't eat too much of it.

多くの人が、サプリでビタミンとミネラルを摂取します。

Many people take vitamins and minerals through supplements.

おいしくて栄養価の高い食べ物を食べるべきです。

You should eat tasty and nutritious foods.

必須栄養素とは何ですか？

What are the essential nutrients?

cut down on 〜を減らす

processed food 加工食品

high in 〜が多い

low in 〜が少ない

calorie-controlled diet カロリーを制限した食事

balanced diet バランスの取れた食事

vegetarian ベジタリアン

overeat 食べ過ぎる、過食する

go on a diet ダイエットを始める

be on a diet ダイエット中である

fast 断食する

skip a meal 食事を抜く

USEFUL SENTENCES

塩分と脂肪分の多い食べ物を減らさないと。	We have to cut down on salty and greasy food.
カキは鉄分が多い。	Oysters are high in iron.
バランスの取れた食事をするのが重要です。	It's important to have a balanced diet.
その歌手はベジタリアンなんだって。	They say the singer is a vegetarian.
彼女、1年中ダイエットしてるんじゃない？	Isn't she on a diet all year long?
断食するのは体にいいのかな、よくないのかな？	Is fasting good for your body or not?

運動、健康管理

`DL 07_03`

work out, exercise
運動する

warm up
準備運動をする

jog ジョギングする
run 走る

go to the gym
スポーツジムへ通う

stretch ストレッチをする

go swimming
泳ぎに行く

do aerobics
エアロビクスをする

do weight training
ウエートトレーニングをする

do squats
スクワットをする

do sit-ups
上体起こしをする

do push-ups
腕立て伏せをする

do circuit training
サーキットトレーニングをする

USEFUL SENTENCES

健康のため、運動してください。	Please exercise for your health.
仕事の合間にストレッチしましょう。	Stretch while you work.
週に3回スポーツジムに通っています。	I go to the gym three times a week.
中年からはウエートトレーニングをすべきです。	From middle age, we should do weight training.
スクワットを毎日しています。	I do squats every day.
腕立て伏せ、何回できる？	How many push-ups can you do?

jump rope
縄跳びをする

do[practice] yoga
ヨガをする

do Pilates
ピラティスをする

meditate
瞑想する

get a massage
マッサージを受ける

watch one's weight 体重に気を付ける
lose weight 体重を減らす、痩せる
gain weight 体重を増やす、太る
quit[stop] smoking 禁煙する
quit[stop] drinking 禁酒する

USEFUL SENTENCES

彼女はヨガを10年間やっています。　She's been doing yoga for 10 years.

痩せなきゃ。5キロくらい。　I have to lose weight. About 5 kilograms.

彼はがんの手術後、禁酒禁煙しました。　He quit smoking and drinking after cancer surgery.

gym スポーツジム
- fitness instructor: ジムのインストラクター
- hire a personal trainer: パーソナルトレーニング (PT) を受ける
- treadmill: ランニングマシン
- weight: ウェートトレーニングの道具
- exercise bike: エアロバイク
- rowing machine: ローイングマシン (ボート漕ぎ運動をする器具)

4 病気、けが

DL 07_04

ache (体全体、頭、胸、心などが) 痛む
hurt, be painful (ある部位が) 痛む
have pain in ～が痛い、～に痛みがある

be sick, be ill
具合が悪い

have a fever
熱がある

have[feel] a chill
悪寒がする

feel dizzy
めまいがする

bleed
血が出る、血を流す

be itchy
かゆい

be sore
(炎症や傷が) 痛い

be swollen
腫れる、むくむ

vomit, throw up
吐く

USEFUL SENTENCES

長い時間運動をしたので、体じゅうが痛い。	I exercised for a long time, and I ache all over.
膝が痛いので、長くは歩けません。	My knee is so painful I cannot walk long.
熱があって悪寒がします。	I have a fever and a chill.
目がかゆくて充血しています。	My eyes are itchy and bloodshot.
今日、何時間も立ち続けていたので、足がむくみました。	My legs are swollen since I've been standing for hours today.
彼は食べたものをすべて吐きました。	He threw up everything he ate.

have a headache	**have a backache**	**have a stomachache**	**catch〔have〕 a cold**
頭が痛い、頭痛がする	腰が痛い	腹が痛い	風邪をひく

have the flu	**have a runny nose**	**cough**	**sneeze**
インフルエンザにかかる	鼻水が出る	咳をする	くしゃみをする

have a sore throat	**have〔get〕diarrhea, have loose bowels**	**have a bloody nose**	**have an allergy to, be allergic to**
喉が痛い	下痢をする	鼻血が出る	～アレルギーである

USEFUL SENTENCES

頭が痛いので、鎮痛剤を飲みました。	I took a painkiller because I had a headache.
母は腰が痛むので、はりをよく打っています。	My mom has a backache and often gets acupuncture treatment.
1年に1回は風邪をひいていると思います。	I think I catch a cold once a year.
数日間、せきが出て喉が痛い。	I've been coughing and have had a sore throat for a few days.
牛乳を飲むといつも下痢をします。	I get diarrhea whenever I drink milk.
彼は卵アレルギーだ。	He's allergic to eggs.

DL 07_05

disease 疾病、病気、疾患
chronic disease 慢性疾患
illness, sickness 病気
disorder (心身機能の)不調、障害
symptom 症状
infection 感染、伝染病
germ 細菌
virus ウイルス
inflammation 炎症
bleeding 出血
rash 発疹、ふきでもの
blister 水ぶくれ、水疱

USEFUL SENTENCES

人類が制圧していない疾病はまだたくさんあります。	There still are many diseases that man has not conquered.
ぜんそくの症状は何ですか？	What are the symptoms of asthma?
感染を防ぐには、手をよく洗うことが重要です。	It is important to wash your hands thoroughly to prevent infection.
この薬は熱を下げて炎症を和らげます。	This medicine reduces fever and relieves inflammation.
食中毒で体じゅうに発疹が出ました。	I have a rash all over my body from food poisoning.

事故、けが

get injured, get hurt, be wounded けがする、負傷する

have a car accident 自動車事故に遭う

get hurt from a fall 転んでけがをする

get a bruise あざができる、打撲する

get a scar 傷を負う

have〔suffer〕burns やけどをする

get a cut on 〜を（刃物で）切る

sprain one's ankle 足首をくじく、捻挫する

wear a cast ギプスをはめる

USEFUL SENTENCES

私の友達は自転車に乗っていてけがをしました。	A friend of mine got hurt while riding a bike.
転んで脚にあざができました。	I fell and got a bruise on my leg.
彼は幼いときにやけどを負いました。	He suffered burns when he was a child.
料理をしていて指を切りました。	I got a cut on my finger while I was cooking.
マイは足首をくじいてギプスをはめなければなりませんでした。	Mai sprained her ankle and had to wear a cast.

DL 07_06

各種の疾病

addiction 中毒
alcoholism アルコール依存症
anemia 貧血
angina 狭心症
appendicitis 虫垂炎
arrhythmia, an irregular pulse 不整脈
arthritis 関節炎
asthma ぜんそく
atopy アトピー
brain tumor 脳腫瘍
cavity 虫歯
cold 風邪
constipation 便秘
dementia 認知症
depression うつ病
diabetes 糖尿病
enteritis 腸炎
food poisoning 食中毒
gastritis 胃炎
heart attack 心臓発作、心臓麻痺
heart disease 心臓病
hemorrhoids, piles 痔
high blood pressure 高血圧
hyperlipidemia 脂質異常症
indigestion 消化不良
influenza, flu インフルエンザ
insomnia 不眠症
leukemia 白血病
malignant tumor 悪性腫瘍
measles 麻疹、はしか
mental illness 精神疾患
migraine 片頭痛
myocardial infarction 心筋梗塞
osteoporosis 骨粗しょう症
panic disorder パニック障害
periodontitis 歯周炎
pneumonia 肺炎
shingles, herpes zoster 帯状疱疹
slipped disc 椎間板ヘルニア
stomach ulcer 胃潰瘍
stroke 脳卒中
tonsillitis へんとう炎
tuberculosis 結核

がん

cancer がん
brain cancer 脳腫瘍
laryngeal cancer 喉頭がん
oral cancer 口腔がん
tongue cancer 舌がん
thyroid cancer 甲状腺がん
esophageal cancer 食道がん
lung cancer 肺がん
breast cancer 乳がん
stomach cancer, gastric cancer 胃がん
liver cancer 肝臓がん
gallbladder cancer 胆のうがん
renal cancer 腎がん
pancreatic cancer すい臓がん
uterine cancer 子宮がん
ovarian cancer 卵巣がん
prostate cancer 前立腺がん
colorectal cancer 大腸がん
rectal cancer 直腸がん
acute myeloid leukemia 急性骨髄性白血病
blood cancer 血液がん
skin cancer 皮膚がん

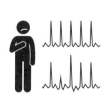

病院、治療、薬

DL 07_07

病院、治療

go to the doctor, go see a doctor
病院へ行く、医者に診察してもらいに行く

examine 検査する、診察する

be treated, get treatment
治療を受ける

heal
治癒する、治る

recover from
〜から回復する

have[get] a shot [an injection]
注射を受ける

be prescribed medicine
薬を処方してもらう

get an IV, put on a drip
点滴を受ける

have[take] a blood test 血液検査を受ける

have[take] a urine test 尿検査を受ける

USEFUL SENTENCES

何日もせきしているね。医者に診察してもらいに行った方がいいよ。	You've been coughing for days. You should go see a doctor.
彼は持病のせいで長い間治療を受けてきました。	He has been treated for a long time because of a chronic disease.
その傷が治るのに数週間かかりました。	It took several weeks for the wound to heal.
病院へ行って注射してもらえばすぐに治るでしょう。	If you go to the hospital and get a shot, you'll be well soon.
片頭痛のため病院で薬を処方してもらいました。	I was prescribed medicine at the hospital for migraine.
血液検査と尿検査を受けました。	I had a blood test and a urine test.

have[take, get] an X-ray
レントゲンを撮る

have[do] a CT scan
CTスキャンをする
have[do] an MRI
MRI撮影をする

have physical therapy
理学療法を受ける

have surgery [an operation]
手術を受ける

get[have, take] a medical check-up[examination]
健診を受ける

enter a hospital, be hospitalized 入院する
leave a hospital 退院する

USEFUL SENTENCES

胸部レントゲン、撮ったことある？	Have you ever had a chest X-ray?
彼女は心臓弁膜手術を受けました。	She had heart valve surgery.
2年に1回、健診を受けています。	I get a medical check-up every second year.

さまざまな診療科

internal medicine 内科	surgery 外科
pediatrics 小児科	obstetrics 産科, gynecology 婦人科
neurology 神経内科	neurosurgery 神経外科
psychiatry 精神科	dermatology 皮膚科
orthopedics 整形外科	plastic surgery 形成外科、美容外科
ophthalmology 眼科	otolaryngology 耳鼻咽喉科
dental clinic, dentist's 歯科	oriental medical clinic 漢方医院

DL 07_08

hospital 病院(病床を備えている総合病院)
clinic 個人[専門]病院、医院
physician 内科医
surgeon 外科医
patient 患者
ambulance 救急車
stethoscope 聴診器
thermometer 体温計
ER(emergency room) 救急治療室
ICU(intensive care unit) 集中治療室
doctor's office, examination room 診察室
operating room 手術室
patient's room 病室
sick ward 入院病棟

USEFUL SENTENCES

近くに歯科医院はありますか？	Is there a dental clinic nearby?
外科医は手術をする医師です。	Surgeons are doctors who perform surgeries.
5分ごとに救急車が救急患者を乗せてきました。	Every five minutes an ambulance came with an emergency patient.
家に体温計を備えた方がいいよ。	You'd better have a thermometer in the house.
昨夜、隣人が救急治療室に運ばれて行きました。	Last night, my neighbor was taken to the emergency room.
集中治療室の患者と面会できますか？	Can I see a patient in the intensive care unit?

薬

take medicine 薬を飲む
prescribe a drug 薬を処方する
pill, tablet 錠剤
liquid medicine 液剤
powder, powdered medicine 粉薬
ointment 軟こう、塗り薬
painkiller 鎮痛剤
fever reducer 解熱剤
digestive medicine 消化剤
antiseptic 消毒薬
pain relief patch 痛み止めパッチ
eye drop 目薬
sleeping pill 睡眠薬

USEFUL SENTENCES

体調が悪い時は、我慢せず薬を飲んで。	When you are sick, don't hold back and do take medicine.
子どもは粉薬を飲むのが苦手です。	Young children have difficulty taking powdered medicine.
鎮痛剤と解熱剤は常備薬です。	Painkillers and fever reducers are household medicines.
睡眠薬がないと眠れません。	I can't sleep without sleeping pills.

first aid kit 救急用品
adhesive bandage 絆創膏
cotton pad 脱脂綿
ice pack 氷のう
thermometer 体温計

bandage 包帯
tweezers ピンセット
gauze ガーゼ
compress 湿布

6 死

DL 07_09

die 死ぬ

pass away 亡くなる

grieve with somebody on the death of ～の死に対して…に弔意を示す

offer one's sympathy for the loss of ～を亡くしたことに対して弔意を示す

Please accept my sympathy for ～にお悔やみ申し上げます

the deceased〔dead〕 故人

dody 遺体

commit suicide, kill oneself 自ら命を絶つ

be brain-dead 脳死状態になる

funeral 葬儀
funeral hall 葬儀場

USEFUL SENTENCES

祖父が亡くなりました。	My grandfather passed away.
お母様のご逝去にお悔やみ申し上げます。	Please accept my sympathy for the loss of your mother.
故人は中学校の恩師でした。	The deceased is my middle school teacher.
その小説家は自ら命を絶ちました。	The novelist committed suicide.
彼は交通事故の後、脳死状態のままです。	He was left brain-dead after a car accident.
その政治家の葬儀には多くの人たちが参列しました。	Numerous people attended the politician's funeral.

coffin
棺

bury 埋葬する
burial 埋葬

grave, tomb
墓、墓所
cemetery 墓地

cremate the body 遺体を火葬する（**cremation** 火葬）
natural burial 自然葬
cinerarium 納骨堂

USEFUL SENTENCES

最近は、ますます多くの人が自然葬を選択して
います。

These days, more and more people choose
a natural burial.

両親が眠る納骨堂に数カ月に１度訪れます。

I visit the cinerarium where my parents are
every few months.

CHAPTER

8

余暇、趣味

Leisure & Hobbies

余暇全般

DL 08_01

be on vacation 休暇中である / **go on vacation** 休暇に出掛ける
go camping キャンプに行く
go on〔have〕a picnic ピクニックに行く
go to〔visit〕a museum/(an art) gallery 博物館／美術館に行く
go to an amusement park/a theme park 遊園地／テーマパークに行く
go hiking 登山に行く
go fishing 釣りに行く
work out, exercise 運動する
go to the gym スポーツジムに行く / **work out at the gym** スポーツジムで運動する
ride a bike〔bicycle〕 自転車に乗る / **go cycling** サイクリングに行く

USEFUL SENTENCES

この夏は、いつ休暇に出掛ける?	When will you go on vacation this summer?
犬を連れてよくピクニックに行きます。	I often go on picnics with my dogs.
時間さえあれば彼は美術館に行きます。	He goes to the art gallery whenever he has time.
いつか一緒に登山に行きましょう。	Let's go hiking together sometime.
空き時間にはスポーツジムで運動をします。	I work out at the gym in my spare time.
川沿いで自転車に乗るのが好きです。	I like riding a bike along the river.

do[practice] yoga ヨガをする
take a walk, go for a walk 散歩する
read a book 本を読む
go to the library 図書館に行く
listen to music 音楽を聴く
go to a concert コンサートに行く
watch TV テレビを見る
watch a movie 映画を見る
go to the movies 映画を見に行く
watch[see] a play/a musical/an opera 演劇／ミュージカル／オペラを見る
play the piano/drums/guitar ピアノ／ドラム／ギターを演奏する

USEFUL SENTENCES

田舎に引っ越してから、毎朝散歩しています。	I take a walk every morning since I moved to the country.
ユミは本を読むのが好きで、図書館にもよく行きます。	Yumi likes reading books, so she often goes to the library.
週末は、映画を見に行くか家でテレビを見ています。	On weekends, I go to the movies or watch TV at home.
趣味？ ミュージカルを見ること。	My hobby? Watching musicals.
週に1回、ドラム演奏をします。	I play the drums once a week.

DL 08_02

take pictures 写真を撮る
draw, paint 絵を描く
make ~ by hand ～を手作りする
make models プラモデルを作る
knit 編み物をする、～を編む
cook 料理する
bake bread/cookies パン／クッキーを焼く
do gardening 庭の手入れ (ガーデニング) をする
arrange flowers 花を生ける
keep[raise] a pet ペットを飼う

USEFUL SENTENCES

絵を描くと心が安らぎます。	Painting makes me feel at ease.
彼は木工品を手作りするのが好きです。	He enjoys making things by hand out of wood.
マフラーを編んで祖母にプレゼントしました。	I knitted a scarf and gave it to my grandmother.
私の最近の趣味はパンを焼くことです。	My hobby these days is baking bread.
多くの英国人がガーデニングを趣味にしているそうです。	They say many British people do gardening as a hobby.
その家族は犬2匹と猫3匹を飼っています。	The family keeps two dogs and three cats.

use social media SNSをする

write a blog post ブログを書く

learn a foreign language 外国語を習う

play mobile games モバイルゲームをする

play board games ボードゲームをする

play cards カードで遊ぶ

sing in a karaoke box カラオケで歌う

go to a club クラブに行く

go to a party パーティーに行く

USEFUL SENTENCES

仕事の後、数時間SNSをしていると思います。 I suppose I use social media for a few hours after work.

少なくとも1日に1回、ブログを書いています。 I write a blog post at least once every day.

彼は退職後、趣味で外国語を習っています。 He's learning a foreign language as a hobby after retirement.

1日中モバイルゲームばかりするつもり？ Are you just going to play mobile games all day?

カラオケに行って歌うと、ストレス解消するよ。 If you sing in a karaoke box, you can relieve your stress.

2 旅行

DL 08_03

take[go on] a trip, travel 旅行をする
take[go on] a one-day trip 日帰り旅行をする (**one-day trip, day trip** 日帰り旅行)
go on a package tour パッケージ旅行をする
go sightseeing 観光する、観光しに行く
travel domestically 国内旅行をする /**domestic travel[trip]** 国内旅行
have[go on] a guided tour ガイドツアーに行く
travel alone 一人旅をする
go on a school trip[an excursion] 修学旅行に行く

**go backpacking,
go on a backpacking trip**
バックパック旅行をする

**travel abroad,
go on an overseas trip**
海外旅行をする

overseas travel[trip] 海外旅行

USEFUL SENTENCES

母はパッケージ旅行に好んで行きます。	My mom prefers to go on package tours.
よく国内旅行をします。毎月どこかに行きます。	I often travel domestically. I go somewhere every month.
バチカンのガイドツアーに行きました。	We had a guided tour of the Vatican.
高校生のとき、修学旅行で京都に行きました。	I went on a school trip to Kyoto when I was in high school.
ヒロコはバックパック旅行で南米に行きました。	Hiroko went on a backpacking trip to South America.
最近、多くの人たちが海外旅行をします。	A lot of people travel abroad these days.

travel by train/car/bus/plane 電車／自動車／バス／飛行機で旅行する
pack one's bags for the trip 旅行の荷造りをする
(travel) itinerary 旅程、旅行の日程表
festival お祭り
souvenir お土産

go on a cruise
クルーズ旅行をする

tourist attraction
観光名所

historic site
名所旧跡

ancient palace
古い宮殿

exchange money
両替する
money exchange 両替

tour guide
旅行[観光]ガイド

USEFUL SENTENCES

イタリア全土を列車で旅行しました。	I traveled all over Italy by train.
旅行の荷造りは済んだ？	Have you packed your bags for the trip?
アラスカ旅行の旅程は組んだ？	Have you made your itinerary for Alaska?
香港の主な観光名所はどこだろう？	Where are the major tourist attractions in Hong Kong?
ソウルには古い宮殿がたくさんあります。	There are many ancient palaces in Seoul.
どこで両替した？	Where did you exchange money?

空港、飛行機

passport パスポート
suitcase スーツケース
baggage 荷物、手荷物
ticket チケット
e-ticket 電子チケット
boarding pass 搭乗券
one-way ticket 片道航空券
round-trip ticket 往復航空券
direct[nonstop] flight 直行便
check-in counter 搭乗手続きカウンター
check in baggage 荷物を預ける
check-in baggage 預入荷物
carry-on bag 機内持ち込み用バッグ
go through passport control 入国審査を受ける
have a security check 保安検査を受ける
duty-free shop 免税店
get ~ tax-free[duty-free] 免税店で~を買う
departure gate 出発ゲート
board[get on] a plane 飛行機に乗る
economy/business/first class エコノミー／ビジネス／ファーストクラス
in-flight service 機内サービス
window seat 窓側の席
aisle seat 通路側の席
land at the airport 空港に着陸する
baggage claim 手荷物受取所
declare ~を税関に申告する
customs 税関
jet lag 時差ぼけ

hotel ホテル

hostel ホステル

guesthouse ゲストハウス

B&B(bed and breakfast) B&B、朝食付き民泊

Airbnb Airbnb、民泊

villa 別荘、休暇用の住宅

resort 休養地、リゾート

motel モーテル

front desk フロント(案内デスク)

receptionist (ホテルの)フロント係

room with a view 眺めのいい部屋

vacancy 空き部屋

complimentary shuttle 無料のシャトルバス

make a reservation 予約する

stay in a hotel ホテルに泊まる

check in チェックインする

check out チェックアウトする

UNIT 3 映画、演劇、ミュージカル

DL 08_05

映画

movie theater 映画館
multiplex 複合型映画館、シネコン
box office チケット売り場、興行収入
audience 観客
director 映画監督
film crew 撮影隊
movie star 映画スター（**actor, actress** 俳優、女優）
cast 出演者
main character 主人公
supporting role 脇役
hero/heroine 男性主人公／女性主人公
villain 悪役
special effects 特殊効果
stuntman/stuntwoman スタントマン／スタントウーマン
screenplay, script 映画の台本、脚本
line せりふ

USEFUL SENTENCES

その映画は興行的に大成功しました。	The movie was a huge box-office success.
その映画は千万人の観客を動員しました。	The movie attracted a total audience of 10 million.
記憶に残るせりふが数多くありました。	There were many memorable lines.

映画のジャンル

drama ドラマ
comedy コメディー
action movie アクション映画
thriller スリラー、サスペンス映画
animation アニメ

period[costume] piece 時代劇
romantic comedy ロマンチックコメディ
science fiction SF
crime drama 犯罪ドラマ
horror movie ホラー映画

play 演劇、戯曲
playwright 脚本家
theater 劇場
stage 舞台
comedy コメディー、喜劇
tragedy 悲劇
performance 公演、演技
costume 衣装
dialogue (劇の)会話の部分
monologue 独白
aside 傍白
act 幕
scene 場、シーン
get[take] a curtain call カーテンコールを受ける
applaud 拍手する
give a standing ovation スタンディングオベーションをする

USEFUL SENTENCES

その戯曲はアイルランドの脚本家によって書かれたものです。	The play was written by an Irish playwright.
その作品は喜劇ですか、悲劇ですか？	Is that a comedy or a tragedy?
そのミュージカルは衣装がとても華やかだ。	The musical has very fancy costumes.
「ハムレット」は5幕から成ります。	"Hamlet" consists of five acts.
俳優たちはカーテンコールを受けました。	The actors got a curtain call.
観客はスタンディングオベーションをしました。	The audience gave a standing ovation.

4 音楽、演奏会

DL 08_06

classical music クラシック音楽
pop(ular) song ポップ・ソング
orchestra オーケストラ、交響楽団
band バンド
melody メロディー、曲調
lyrics 歌詞

choir
合唱団、聖歌隊

solo
ソロ

musician
ミュージシャン、音楽家

singer-songwriter
シンガーソングライター

USEFUL SENTENCES

クラシック音楽はあまりよく知りません。 I don't know much about classical music.

ヒロシは市立交響楽団でバイオリンを弾いています。 Hiroshi plays the violin in the city orchestra.

彼はロックバンドでベースギターを弾いています。 He plays the bass guitar in a rock band.

この歌の歌詞がとても好きです。 I love the lyrics of this song.

高校の合唱団の団員でした。 I was a member of the high school choir.

イギリスの歌手、アデルはシンガーソングライターです。 British singer Adele is a singer-songwriter.

listen to music
音楽を聴く

sing a song
歌を歌う

play the ~
(楽器を)演奏する

compose 作曲する
composer 作曲家

conduct 指揮する
conductor 指揮者

perform 演奏する、公演する
busk バスキング(路上ライブ)をする

go to a concert
コンサートに行く

book[buy] a ticket チケットを予約[購入]する
call for an encore アンコールをする
applaud 拍手をする
give a standing ovation スタンディングオベーションをする

USEFUL SENTENCES

ジュンは趣味でピアノを弾いています。	Jun plays the piano as a hobby.
私たちは学園祭で演奏する予定です。	We're going to perform at the school festival.
そのミュージシャンは原宿周辺でよく路上ライブをします。	The musician often busks in the Harajuku area.
BTSのコンサートチケットは予約できた？	Did you manage to book tickets for the BTS concert?
聴衆がアンコールをしました。	The audience called for an encore.
彼らはそのシンガーに拍手をしました。	They applauded the singer.

5 本

DL 08_07

author, writer 著者、作者、作家
title 題名
publish 出版する、刊行する
publisher, publishing company 出版社
editor 編集者
edition (本の)版
hard cover ハードカバー
paperback ペーパーバック
plot (小説などの)粗筋
character 登場人物
page-turner 読みだしたらやめられない本

e-book 電子書籍
e-reader 電子書籍リーダー

audio book
オーディオブック

bookmark
しおり

USEFUL SENTENCES

その作家の新作が来月出版されます。	The author's new book will be published next month.
ついに出版社と契約した！	I finally signed a contract with a publishing company!
その本の初版をどうしても手に入れたいです。	I'm dying to get the first edition of the book.
『ライ麦畑でつかまえて』は、どんな粗筋？	What's the plot of "The Catcher in the Rye"?
その小説で、好きな登場人物は誰？	Who is your favorite character in the novel?
電子書籍に、まだ慣れていません。	I'm not used to e-books yet.

novel 小説

fiction フィクション、小説

self-help book 自己啓発本

fable 寓話

science fiction SF

detective novel 探偵小説

fantasy ファンタジー

autobiography 自伝

encyclopedia 百科事典

comic (book) 漫画本

travel guidebook 旅行ガイドブック

magazine 雑誌

newspaper (headline, article, editorial)
新聞 (見出し、記事、社説)

essay エッセー、随筆

nonfiction ノンフィクション

fairy tale おとぎ話

collection of poems 詩集

crime novel 犯罪小説

romance 恋愛小説

biography 伝記

travel essay 旅行記

dictionary 辞書

cookbook 料理本

textbook 教科書

USEFUL SENTENCES

その本はフィクションですか、ノンフィクションですか？　Is the book fiction or nonfiction?

自己啓発本がたくさん売れた時期がありました。　There was a time when self-help books were selling a lot.

ダイスケは探偵小説と犯罪小説をたくさん読んでいます。　Daisuke reads a lot of detective novels and crime novels.

書店
online bookstore インターネット書店
secondhand bookstore 古書店
independent bookstore 個人経営の書店
large[grand] bookstore 大型書店

6 テレビ、エンターテインメント

`DL 08_08`

cable TV ケーブルテレビ
IPTV(Internet Protocol Television) IPTV
broadcasting station[company] 放送局、放送会社
show, program 番組
episode エピソード(1話分)
season (テレビ番組の)シーズン
host 司会
weather forecaster 気象予報士
TV commercial テレビコマーシャル
commercial break コマーシャルの時間
celebrity culture セレブ文化
household name 誰でもよく知っている名前、有名人

satellite TV
衛星テレビ

channel
チャンネル

(news) anchor
ニュース番組のアンカー、
キャスター

reporter
記者、レポーター

USEFUL SENTENCES

その放送局はドキュメンタリー専門だ。	The broadcasting station specializes in documentaries.
そのドラマの昨日のエピソード、見逃しちゃった！	I missed yesterday's episode of the drama!
その司会者、知らない人いる？	Is there anyone who doesn't know the host?
そのニュースキャスターは、インタビューがとても上手なことで有名です。	The news anchor is famous for being very good at interviews.
あの記者、どうして言葉に詰まっているのだろう？	Why is that reporter stammering?

news ニュース
documentary ドキュメンタリー
drama ドラマ
series シリーズ物、連続ドラマ
soap opera 連続メロドラマ
sitcom シットコム
comedy コメディー
period drama 時代劇
talk show トークショー
quiz show クイズ番組
cartoon 漫画、アニメ
reality TV show リアリティー番組
children's show 子ども番組
cooking show 料理番組
shopping channel ショッピング・チャンネル
talent show 才能発掘番組

---

soap opera

soap operaは、主に昼間、主婦たちを対象に放送されるテレビやラジオの連続ドラマを指します。感情に訴えたり、扇情的だったり、軽快な内容で構成されています。soap operaという名前が付いたのは、初期の頃、石けん業者がこのドラマにコマーシャルを打っていたためです。

テレビに関連する表現
• turn on the TV: テレビをつける
• turn off the TV: テレビを消す
• turn up the volume: ボリュームを上げる
• turn down the volume: ボリュームを下げる
• change channels: チャンネルを替える

7 スポーツ

DL 08_09

play ~

soccer サッカーをする

basketball バスケットボールをする

volleyball バレーボールをする

table tennis 卓球をする

baseball 野球をする

badminton バドミントンをする

tennis テニスをする

golf ゴルフをする

do ~

boxing ボクシングをする

gymnastics 体操をする

long jump 走り幅跳びをする

judo 柔道をする

high jump 走り高跳びをする

bungee jump バンジージャンプをする

* **run a marathon** マラソンをする

USEFUL SENTENCES

世界中の男の子が、よくサッカーをします。	Boys all over the world play soccer a lot.
高校生の頃、バスケットボールをしていました。	I used to play basketball when I was in high school.
卓球をしたことはありますか？	Have you ever played table tennis?
息子は7歳から柔道をしています。	My child has been doing judo since he was 7.
いくらお金を積まれてもバンジージャンプはできません。	I can't do a bungee jump no matter how much money I'll be given.
70歳を過ぎても、彼はまだマラソンをしています。	He's over 70, but he still runs marathons.

go ~

mountain climbing 登山をする

rock climbing ロッククライミングをする

cycling サイクリングをする(に行く)

skating スケートをする(に行く)

skateboarding スケートボードをする(に行く)

skiing スキーをする(に行く)

snowboarding スノーボードをする(に行く)

horse riding 乗馬をする(に行く)

canoeing カヌーをする(に行く)

skydiving スカイダイビングをする(に行く)

paragliding パラグライディングをする(に行く)

diving ダイビングをする(に行く)

scuba diving スキューバダイビングをする(に行く)

snorkeling シュノーケリングをする(に行く)

USEFUL SENTENCES

ヨウジは今度の土曜日、ロッククライミングをするんだって。	Yoji said he's going to go rock climbing this Saturday.
冬にはときどきスキーをしに行きます。	I sometimes go skiing in the winter.

自転車に関する表現
- ride a bike: 自転車に乗る
- get on/off a bike: 自転車に乗る／自転車から降りる
- cycling trail: (自然の中の) 自転車コース
- bicycle lane: (市内の) 自転車専用レーン
- mountain bike: マウンテンバイク
- cycling helmet: 自転車用ヘルメット
- lock: ロック、鍵
- handlebar: ハンドル
- saddle: サドル
- bike rack: (駐輪用の) 自転車固定装置、バイクラック

キャンプ、海水浴、サーフィン

DL 08_10

campsite, campground
キャンプ場、野営地

pitch a tent
テントを張る

build a fire
火を起こす

folding chair
折りたたみいす

flashlight
懐中電灯

go camping キャンプに行く
camping car, motorhome, camper, caravan キャンピングカー
sleeping bag 寝袋
air mattress, air bed エアーマット（空気を注入するマットレス）
camping stove キャンプ用コンロ
bug repellent 防虫剤

USEFUL SENTENCES

最近はあちこちにキャンプ場があります。 There are campsites in many places these days.

テントを張るのは思っていたより難しい。 It is more difficult to pitch a tent than I thought.

折りたたみテーブルといすを広げて食事を しました。 We spread out our folding table and chairs and ate our meals.

彼は家族とキャンプに行くため、 キャンピングカーを買った。 He bought a camping car to go camping with his family.

エアーマット使ったことありますか？ Have you ever used an air mattress?

キャンプに行くときは、防虫剤を持って いかなければなりません。 When you go camping, you have to take bug repellent.

swim〔bathe〕 in the sea
海水浴をする

swimsuit
女性用水着

swimming trunks
男性用水着

sunbathing
日光浴

deck chair
デッキチェア

swim ring
浮き輪

go surfing
サーフィンをに行く

snorkeling
シュノーケリング

scuba-diving
スキューバダイビング

lifeguard
水難救助員、ライフガード

sunscreen 日焼け止め剤

jet ski ジェットスキー

wet suit ウェットスーツ

life preserver〔jacket/vest〕
(救命胴衣などの) 救命用具

USEFUL SENTENCES

久しく海水浴に行っていないね。
It's been a long time since I swam in the sea.

ニースのビーチには、日光浴をする人たちがたくさんいました。
There were a lot of people sunbathing on the beaches in Nice.

デッキチェアに座って本を読みます。
I read a book sitting on the deck chair.

ライフガードが溺れた人を救助しました。
The lifeguard saved the drowning man.

ビーチに行くときは、日焼け止めをしっかり塗らなければなりません。
You have to cover yourself with sunscreen thoroughly when you go to the beach.

仕事、経済

Jobs & Economy

1 会社全般

DL 09_01

company, firm 会社
large[big, major] company 大企業
conglomerate 巨大複合企業
headquarters 本社、本部
branch 支社
subsidiary 子会社
affiliate 系列会社
subcontractor 下請け企業
chairperson 会長
president 社長
executive, director 幹部、重役
department 部署

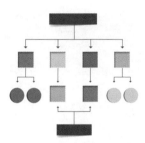

USEFUL SENTENCES

多くの若者が大企業に就職しようとします。
Many young people want to get a job in a large company.

韓国の巨大複合企業は「財閥（チェボル）」と呼ばれます。
The Korean conglomerate is called "chaebol."

アマゾンの本社はシアトルにあります。
Amazon's headquarters is in Seattle.

兄はトヨタの下請け企業で働いています。
My brother works for a Toyota subcontractor.

彼はその会社に入社して20年後に重役になりました。
He became an executive 20 years after joining the company.

マーケティング部で働き始めました。
I started working in the marketing department.

board of directors 取締役会
CEO 最高経営責任者 (**Chief Executive Officer**)
COO 最高執行責任者 (**Chief Operating Officer**)
CIO 最高情報責任者 (**Chief Information Officer**)
CFO 最高財務責任者 (**Chief Financial Officer**)
CTO 最高技術責任者 (**Chief Technology Officer**)

---

employer 雇用主、雇い主
employee 被雇用者、従業員
supervisor 上司、監督者
assistant 助手、アシスタント
intern インターン (**internship** インターン生)
secretary 秘書

USEFUL SENTENCES

その会社の最高経営責任者はインド系米国人です。 The company's CEO is an Indian-American man.

その会社は100人を超す従業員がいます。 The company has more than 100 employees.

広告会社でインターンとして働きました。 I worked as an intern at an advertising company.

職位の英語表現例
会長、取締役会議長: chairperson
副会長: vice chairperson
最高経営責任者、社長: CEO, president
副社長: vice president
専務: senior managing director
常務: managing director
部長: general manager, department head
副部長: deputy general manager
チーム長: team manager
課長: manager, section chief
課長補佐: assistant manager

DL 09_02

wage 賃金、給料
payday 給料日
pay raise 昇給
pay cut 減給

bonus
賞与金

labor force
労働力

---

employee welfare 従業員の福利厚生
workday, working day 勤務日
business day 営業日
working[office] hours 勤務時間
business hours 営業時間
labor union 労働組合
go on strike ストライキする

USEFUL SENTENCES

うちの会社の給料日は毎月20日です。	Our company's payday is the 20th of every month.
今年の昇給は期待できないと思います。	I don't think I can expect a pay raise this year.
うちの会社は従業員の福利厚生が行き届いています。	Our company has good employee welfare.
今日は勤務日ではありません。	Today is not a working day.
あなたの会社の勤務時間はどうなってますか？	What are your working hours?
労働組合はストライキを決定しました。	The labor union decided to go on strike.

management
管理、運営、経営

organization
組織

leadership
リーダーシップ

teamwork
チームワーク

interpersonal skills
対人スキル

project management
プロジェクト管理

time management
時間管理

decision making
意思決定

problem solving
問題解決

data analysis
データ分析

negotiation
交渉

USEFUL SENTENCES

リーダーシップとチームワークが、組織の成功には重要です。

Leadership and teamwork are important for an organization to succeed.

対人スキルも仕事では重要です。

Interpersonal skills are also important at work.

意思決定は十分な情報を基に行われるべきです。

Decision making should be based on sufficient information.

部署
management: 管理、運営
PR(public relations): 広報
IT(information technology): IT（情報技術）
production: 生産
purchasing: 購買

HR(human resources): 人事
R&D(research and development): 研究開発
accounts/finance: 会計／財務
marketing: マーケティング
sales: 営業、販売

さまざまな職業

accountant 会計士、会計員

actor 俳優

architect 建築家

artist 芸術家

astronaut 宇宙飛行士

astronomer 天文学者

athlete スポーツ選手

babysitter ベビーシッター

bank clerk 銀行員

banker 銀行の役員

barber 理髪師

book editor 書籍編集者

bus driver バス運転手

business person ビジネスマン

butcher 精肉店主

carpenter 大工

cartoonist 漫画家

cashier 現金出納係、レジ係

chef 料理人

civil officer 公務員

cleaner 清掃員

comedian コメディアン

composer 作曲家

construction worker 建設労働者

dentist 歯科医

doctor 医師

electrician 電気技師

engineer エンジニア

farmer 農業経営者

fashion designer ファッションデザイナー

firefighter 消防士

flight attendant (旅客機の)客室乗務員

hairdresser 美容師

interior designer インテリアデザイナー

interpreter 通訳

janitor 守衛、建物の管理人

journalist ジャーナリスト、記者

judge 判事

lawyer 弁護士

librarian 司書

mechanic 整備士

model モデル

movie director 映画監督

musician 音楽家

novelist 小説家

nurse 看護師

office worker 事務員

oriental medicine practioner 漢方医

painter 画家

paramedic 救急医療隊員

part-timer 非常勤職員、パートタイマー、アルバイト

pharmacist 薬剤師

photographer 写真家

physician 内科医

pilot パイロット

plumber 配管工

police officer 警察官

professor 教授

prosecutor 検事

psychiatrist 精神科医

psychologist 心理学者

receptionist 受付係

reporter 報道記者、レポーター

scientist 科学者

sculptor 彫刻家

security guard 警備員、保安要員

server (レストランの)接客係

singer 歌手

store clerk 店員

storekeeper, shopkeeper 小売商人、店主

surgeon 外科医

taxi driver タクシー運転手

teacher 教師

tour guide 旅行(観光)ガイド

train driver 電車の運転手

translator 翻訳家

travel agent 旅行会社の社員

TV director テレビディレクター

TV writer テレビ放送作家

vet, veterinarian 獣医

writer 作家

go to work
出勤する

work from home
在宅勤務をする

get approval from
〜の承認[決裁]をもらう

make a weekly plan
週計画を立てる

finish work 仕事を終える
leave work[the office], get off work 退勤する
work full-time, be a full-time worker 常勤で働く
work part-time, be a part-time worker 非常勤[パート／アルバイト]で働く
temporary worker 臨時社員
contract worker 契約社員
work in shifts シフト制で働く
be in charge of 〜を任されている、担当している

USEFUL SENTENCES

在宅勤務ができたらいいのに。	I wish I could work from home.
それはチーム長の決裁をもらう必要があります。	It needs to get approval from our team manager.
ふだんは何時に退勤しますか？	What time do you usually get off work?
彼女は常勤で働いています。	She works full-time.
契約社員です。	I am a contract worker.
このプロジェクトを担当してもらいたいです。	I want you to be in charge of this project.

have a meeting
会議をする

attend a meeting
会議に参加する

wrap up the meeting
会議をまとめる

give a presentation
発表する、
プレゼンテーションをする

reach a deal
合意に至る

work overtime
残業する

be promoted
昇進する

promotion 昇進

**go on
a business trip**
出張に行く

have a day off 1日休暇を取る
take an annual vacation 年次休暇を取る
call in sick 病欠の電話を入れる
go on maternity/paternity leave 出産育児休暇に入る
be on maternity/paternity leave 出産育児休暇中だ

USEFUL SENTENCES

2時に会議します。

We'll have a meeting at two o'clock.

来週、社長の前でプレゼンテーションをしなければなりません。

I have to give a presentation in front of the president next week.

彼は部長に昇進しました。

He was promoted to the department head.

明日、ニューヨークへ出張に行きます。

I'm going on a business trip to New York tomorrow.

1日休暇を取って健診を受けました。

I had a day off and got a medical check-up.

来月、出産育児休暇に入ります。

I'm going on maternity leave next month.

169

就職、退社、失業

DL 09_06

就職

apply for a job 仕事に応募する
submit a résumé[CV(curriculum vitae)] 履歴書を提出する
have[do] a job interview 面接を受ける
get a job 仕事を得る
join[enter] a company 入社する
post a job opening 求人広告を出す (**job opening** 職の空き)
headhunt 人材をスカウトする
(**headhunter** ヘッドハンター, **headhunting** 人材スカウト)
job seeker 求職者
job offer 仕事の依頼[提案]
job opportunity 就職の機会
qualifications 資格(条件)

USEFUL SENTENCES

今まで50件以上の仕事に応募しました。	I've applied for over 50 jobs so far.
履歴書を提出してください。	Please submit your résumé.
明日その会社の面接を受けます。	I'm having a job interview with the company tomorrow.
うちの会社に職の空きが出たら連絡します。	I'll contact you if there's a job opening in our company.
多くの求職者が毎日就職フェアに来ます。	Many job seekers come to the job fair every day.
その仕事の資格条件は何ですか?	What are the qualifications for the job?

quit one's job 会社を辞める
lose one's job 職を失う
get fired, be fired 解雇される (**fire** ～を解雇する)
be laid off 解雇される (**lay someone off** ～を解雇する)
be unemployed[jobless, out of work] 失業状態である
unemployment 失業
unemployed[jobless] person 失業者

retire 引退する (**retirement** 引退)
retired person 退職者、引退した人
receive one's pension 年金をもらう
receive severance pay 退職金をもらう

USEFUL SENTENCES

体調が悪く会社を辞めました。	I quit my job because I was in bad health.
彼は賄賂を受け取って解雇されました。	He was fired for taking bribes.
その会社は100人を超す従業員を解雇しました。	The company laid off more than 100 workers.
彼女の夫は数年前から失業しています。	Her husband has been unemployed for several years.
何歳で引退しましたか？	How old were you when you retired?
65歳から年金を受け取る予定です。	I'm going to receive my pension from 65.

4 経済全般

DL 09_07

economy 経済、景気
industry 産業、業界
enterprise, company, firm 企業、会社
corporation 企業、法人
demand 需要
supply 供給
production 生産
product 生産物、商品、製品
manufacture 製造[生産]する、製造、生産
manufacturer 製造会社
goods 製品、商品
service サービス

USEFUL SENTENCES

世界経済が不況に陥っています。	The world economy is in recession.
彼は旅行業に従事しています。	He's in the tourism industry.
価格は供給と需要によって決まります。	Prices are determined by supply and demand.
新商品の開発に携わっています。	I work on developing new products.
このスマートフォンは韓国で製造されたと書いてあります。	It says that this smartphone was manufactured in Korea.
その会社は家具製造会社です。	The company is a furniture manufacturer.

supplier 供給業者

vendor 販売業者、露天商

partner 提携企業

subcontractor 下請け業者

profit 利益

loss 損失

have a gain〔surplus〕, be in the black 黒字になる

be in deficit, be in the red 赤字を出す

income 収入、所得

expense 支出、費用

revenue (政府などの)歳入、(企業などの)収益

cost(s) 費用、経費

expenditure 支出

USEFUL SENTENCES

その供給業者がさらに安い価格を提示しました。	The supplier offered a lower price.
彼はインターネットショッピングモールの運営で大きな利益を上げました。	He made a huge profit from running an internet shopping mall.
貿易収支は何年間も黒字です。	The trade balance has been in the black for years.
低所得者のためのさまざまな福祉政策が実施されています。	Various welfare policies are carried out for low-income people.
収入と支出のバランスを取る必要があります。	You have to balance your income with your expenses.
その会社はどのように経費を減らせるでしょうか？	How can the company cut costs?

asset 資産
debt 負債、借金
liability 負債、債務
monopoly 独占、専売
investment 投資（**invest** 投資する）
transaction 取引
economic downturn 景気低迷
economic recovery 景気回復
recession, depression 景気後退、不況
economic boom 好景気
up-phase （経済の）好況期
inflation インフレ
deflation デフレ

USEFUL SENTENCES

その会社は資産管理サービスを提供しています。	The company provides asset management services.
彼は賭け事で多額の借金を抱えています。	He is heavily in debt for gambling.
全財産を不動産に投資したのですか？	Did you invest all your money in real estate?
景気低迷が続くと思いますか？	Do you think the economic downturn is going to last?
好景気の間は、生産性、売上、収入のすべてが増加しました。	During the economic boom, productivity, sales and income all increased.
インフレとは、一定期間にわたり、商品やサービスの価格が上昇することです。	Inflation is the increase in the prices of goods and services over a period of time.

inflation rate 物価上昇率
price index 物価指数
price stabilization 物価[価格]安定
price fluctuation 物価[価格]変動
capital 資本
labor 労働
wholesale 卸売
retail sale 小売
bankruptcy 破産
go bankrupt 破産する

USEFUL SENTENCES

これは、住宅価格変動の現況をグラフにしたものです。	This is a graph of the current state of housing price fluctuations.
会社を興すには資本がいくら必要ですか？	How much capital do you need to set up a company?
彼が経営していた建設会社は破産しました。	The construction company he was running went bankrupt.

さまざまな業界

advertising 広告	agriculture, farming 農業
construction 建設	education 教育
electronics エレクトロニクス	entertainment エンターテインメント
fashion ファッション	finance 金融
fishing 漁業	forestry 林業
healthcare 医療	journalism ジャーナリズム
livestock farming 畜産業	manufacturing 製造
mining 鉱業	pharmaceutical 製薬
real estate 不動産	shipping 海運
tourism 観光	transportation 運送

金融

finance
金融、財務、財政

currency
通貨

cash 現金
(**coin** 硬貨, **bill** 紙幣)

check
小切手

credit card
クレジットカード
debit card
デビットカード

ATM (automatic teller machine)
現金自動預払機

PIN (number)
個人暗証番号

mobile banking
モバイルバンキング

bankbook 通帳
bank account number 銀行の口座番号
online banking オンラインバンキング

USEFUL SENTENCES

どの省が国家財政を運営していますか？	Which department manages the national finances?
ヨーロッパの大半の国は、単一通貨、ユーロを使用しています。	Most European countries use a single currency, the euro.
クレジットカードとデビットカードはどう違うの？	How are credit cards and debit cards different?
その地下鉄駅にはATMがありますか？	Is there an ATM at the subway station?
最近、モバイルバンキングが多用されています。	People use mobile banking a lot these days.
銀行の口座番号を教えてください。	Please let me know your bank account number.

interest 利子

interest rate 利率

open/close a bank account 銀行口座を開設する／解約する

save money 貯金する

get into debt 借金を負う

deposit money 預金する

withdraw money 預金を引き出す

remit, send[transfer] money 送金する

put ~ into a fixed deposit account ～を定期預金口座に入れる

put[pay] ~ into an installment savings account ～を積立預金口座に入れる

get a bank loan, get a loan from the bank 銀行貸付を受ける

take out/pay off a mortgage 担保貸付を受ける／返済する

USEFUL SENTENCES

最近は預金の利率がわずか0.1パーセントほどです。	These days, the interest rate on deposits is only about 0.1 percent.
今後利用しない銀行口座は解約してください。	Close the bank account that you don't use any more.
費用は彼に送金してください。	Please remit the expenses to him.
まとまったお金を受け取ると、定期預金口座に入れています。	When I get a large sum of money, I put it into a fixed deposit account.
毎月3万円ずつ積立預金口座に入れています。	I pay 30,000 yen into an installment savings account every month.
銀行から貸付を受けるのがだんだん難しくなっている。	It's getting harder and harder to get a loan from the bank.

株式

stock exchange
証券[株式]取引所

buy stocks
株を買う

sell stocks
株を売る

**make/lose
money in stocks**
株でもうける／損する

税金

pay tax
税金を払う

**get[receive]
a tax refund**
税金の還付を受ける

tax cut
減税

tax hike
増税

**deduction of
tax**
税金控除

USEFUL SENTENCES

東京証券取引所はどこですか？	Where is the Tokyo Stock Exchange?
株を買ったことはありますか？	Have you ever bought stocks?
おじは株で大金を失いました。	My uncle lost a lot of money in stocks.
多くの人たちが税金を払っていません。	There are a lot of people who don't pay taxes.
どうすれば税金の還付が受けられますか？	How do I get a tax refund?
減税は消費者マインドの向上に役立ちます。	Tax cuts can help boost consumer sentiment.

Many job seekers come to the job fair every day.

JOB

I've applied for over 50 jobs so far.

10

ショッピング

——

Shopping

さまざまな店

`DL 10_01`

market
市場

traditional market 昔ながらの市場
local market 地元の市場

street market
露天市

department store
百貨店、デパート

shopping mall
ショッピングモール

supermarket
スーパーマーケット

convenience store
コンビニ

flea market フリーマーケット
grocery (store) 食料品店、食料雑貨店

USEFUL SENTENCES

地方自治体は地元の市場の活性化に努めている。	Local governments are trying to boost local markets.
露天市を見て回るのが楽しかったです。	It was fun to look around the street market.
近所にデパートやショッピングモールがあるでしょうか？	Is there a department store or a shopping mall nearby?
最近、コンビニには何でもある。	There's everything in convenience stores these days.
フリーマーケットでいい品物をいくつか買いました。	I bought some nice things at the flea market.
食料品店に行って酢とキュウリを買ってきて。	Go to the grocery store and get some vinegar and cucumbers.

**baker's,
bakery**

ベーカリー、製菓店

**butcher shop,
the butcher's**

精肉店

fish dealer

鮮魚店

**fruit
shop[store]**

フルーツパーラー

rice store[shop]

米穀店

furniture store

家具店

**electronics store,
electrical appliances store**

電器店

**clothing
store[shop]**

衣料品店

**lingerie shop[store],
underwear shop[store]**

下着店

shoe shop[store]

靴店

**jewelry
store**

宝石店

USEFUL SENTENCES

ベーカリーの前を歩くと、いい匂いがします。	It smells good when I walk past the bakery.
精肉店で豚肉を600グラム買いました。	I bought 600 grams of pork at the butcher's.
その通りには多くの家具店があります。	There are many furniture stores on the street.
新しいテレビを買う必要があるので、電器店に行く予定です。	I need to buy a new TV so I'm going to the electronics store.
下着店でパンティーと靴下を買いました。	I bought some panties and socks at the underwear store.
以前ここに宝石店がありました。	There used to be a jewelry store here.

bookstore
書店

stationery shop[store]
文具店

flower[florist] shop
生花店

hardware store
金物店

pharmacy, chemist's
薬局

drugstore
ドラッグストア

barber shop 理髪店
beauty salon, beauty parlor, hair salon 美容院
real estate agency 不動産仲介業者
laundry, dry cleaner's クリーニング店

USEFUL SENTENCES

地元の書店がなくて残念です。	I'm sorry there aren't any local bookstores.
めいは文具店に行くのが好きです。	My niece likes to go to the stationery shop.
金物店でモップを売っていますか？	Do they sell mops in the hardware store?
この辺りで、日曜日に開いている薬局はありますか？	Is there a pharmacy in this neighborhood that opens on Sunday?
今日、美容院に行って髪を切ってもらう予定です。	I'm going to the beauty parlor to get my hair cut today.
この辺りには不動産仲介業者が多数あります。	There are a lot of real estate agencies around here.

cosmetics 化粧品
menswear 紳士服
womenswear 婦人服
children's wear 子ども服
lingerie 下着
sportswear スポーツウエア
bags バッグ
shoes 靴
toys 玩具
stationery 文具
electrical appliances, home appliances 家電製品
home furnishings インテリア、家具
kitchenware キッチン用品
food court フードコート
duty-free shop 免税店
customer service 顧客サービス

2 ショッピング全般

DL 10_03

window-shop, go window shopping ウインドーショッピングする
shop around あちこちの店を見て回る
be out of stock 在庫が切れている
bargain[haggle] (over) ~の値段交渉する
give a discount 値引きする
pay in installments 分割で買う
exchange A for B AをBと交換する
get a refund (on) ~の払い戻しを受ける

try on
~を試着する

be on sale
販売中である、セール中である

pay in cash
現金で払う

**pay by
credit card**
クレジットカードで払う

USEFUL SENTENCES

掘り出し物を探してあちこちの店を見て回りました。

I shopped around for bargains.

Mサイズは在庫が切れています。

M size is out of stock.

母は市場で物を買うとき、値段交渉します。

My mother bargains when she buys things in the market.

これの払い戻しを受けたいです。

I'd like to get a refund on this.

これ、試着できますか？

Can I try this on?

お支払いは現金ですか、カードですか？

Would you like to pay in cash or by credit card?

operating[business] hours 営業時間
fixed price 定価
special offer 特価提供
shelves 陳列棚
fitting room 試着室
receipt 領収証

price tag
値札

promote 販促する
promotion
販促

shopping cart
ショッピングカート

basket
かご

shopping bag
ショッピングバッグ、
買い物袋

clerk 店員
cashier
レジ、レジ係

cash register
レジ、
金銭登録器

customer
顧客

checkout (counter)
レジカウンター

USEFUL SENTENCES

そのデパートの営業時間は何時ですか？	What are the business hours of the department store?
ここではそれらを定価で販売します。	We sell them here at a fixed price.
試着室はどこですか？	Where is the fitting room?
ショッピングカートがありません。	There's no shopping cart.
自分のショッピングバッグを持ち歩いています。	I carry my shopping bag with me.
レジカウンターはどちらですか？	Which way is the checkout counter?

オンラインショッピング、個人輸入の用語

DL 10_04

オンラインショッピング

internet shopping mall インタネットショッピングモール
create an account アカウントを作る (**account** アカウント)
membership 会員(資格)

log in to, sign in to ～にログインする
log out of, sign out of ～からログアウトする

category ショッピングカテゴリー
add to one's cart[bag] カートに入れる
add to one's wish list 欲しい物リストに加える

order 注文する
enter a shipping address 配送先住所を入力する
shipping information 配送情報(受取人の名前、住所、電話番号、Eメールアドレスなど)
payment information 決済情報(決済方法、カードの種類など)
continue to payment, proceed to checkout 決済を進める

order number 注文番号
tracking number 送り状番号
shipping and handling charge, delivery charge 送料
charge ~ for shipping (and handling) 送料を~に請求する
send ~ by C. O. D. (cash[collect] on delivery) ~を着払いで送る
deliver ~ for free ~を無料で配送する
free shipping 送料無料
return item 返却品
choose items to return 返品する品物を選択する

 個人輸入　

overseas purchase 海外購入
foreign site 海外サイト
order from abroad 海外からの注文
Black Friday ブラックフライデー（11月の第4金曜日、大規模セールを実施する）
Cyber Monday
サイバーマンデー（ブラックフライデーの次の月曜日、大規模セールを実施する）
Boxing Day ボクシングデー（クリスマスの翌日、セールを実施）
shipping address 届け先住所（個人輸入の場合は通常、受け取り代行先の住所）
billing address 請求書送付先住所（カード発給住所、個人輸入の場合は通常、受け取り代行先の住所）
sales tax 海外から商品を購入時に賦課される消費税
back order 商品の在庫切れにより製造元に注文している状態（商品が入荷されれば配送）
off load 航空会社の事情などにより予定の便に荷物が乗らなかった
return label 返品ラベル（返品時に印刷後、箱の側面に貼らなければならない）

11

国家

Nation

1 政治

politics 政治、政治活動

politician (選挙により選ばれた) 政治家

statesman (経験豊富で指導力のある) 政治家

political power 政治権力、政治勢力

government 政府、政治 [統治] 体制、行政

administration 行政、行政府

jurisdiction 司法権

judiciary 司法府

legislation 立法行為、法律制定

legislature 立法府

legislator, lawmaker 立法者、国会議員

USEFUL SENTENCES

政治は私たちの生活と密接な関係があるので、関心を持つべきです。

Politics is closely related to our lives, so we should pay attention to it.

友達のお父さんは有名な政治家でした。

My friends' father was a famous politician.

国家権力は行政府、立法府、司法府に分けられます。

State power is divided into the administration, the legislature and the judiciary.

わが国では総理大臣が行政府の長です。

In our country, the prime minister is the head of the administration.

司法府の長は最高裁判所の長官です。

The head of the judiciary is the Chief Justice of the Supreme Court.

国会が行うことは、立法、つまり法律を制定することです。

What the Diet does is legislation, that is to enact laws.

Diet 国会

member of the Diet 国会議員

House of Representatives 衆議院

House of Councilors 参議院

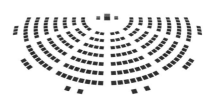

political party 政党

ruling party 与党

opposition party 野党

progressive 進歩的な、進歩主義の

conservative 保守的な

liberal 自由主義の、進歩主義の、進歩的な

coalition 連立

USEFUL SENTENCES

与党とは政権を握っている党です。

The ruling party is the party that holds the power.

野党は政府を精査し説明責任を課すべきです。

The opposition party should scrutinize the government and hold it accountable.

彼は進歩的ですか、保守的ですか？

Is he progressive or conservative?

democracy 民主主義
democratic 民主主義の、民主的な

republic
共和制（共和国）

dictatorship
独裁制

monarchy
君主制

anarchy
無政府状態

parliamentary democracy 議会制民主主義
totalitarianism 全体主義（**totalitarian** 全体主義の）
socialism 社会主義（**socialist** 社会主義者、社会主義の）
capitalism 資本主義（**capitalist** 資本主義者、資本家）
communism 共産主義（**communist** 共産主義者、共産主義の）

USEFUL SENTENCES

全体主義体制では、個人は集団のためにだけ存在します。	In a totalitarian regime, individuals exist only for groups.
資本主義は政治体制ではなく経済体制です。	Capitalism is not a political system but an economic system.
効果的な教育政策を確立する必要があります。	It is necessary to establish an effective education policy.
その国会議員が今年、最も多くの法案を発議しました。	The lawmaker proposed the most bills this year.

establish a policy 政策を確立する
propose a bill 法案を発議する
pass a bill 法案を通過させる[可決する]
appoint 任命する

prime minister 首相、総理大臣
minister 大臣
vice minister 副大臣
cabinet 内閣

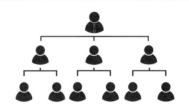

行政機関

内閣府	Cabinet Office
国家公安委員会（警察庁）	National Public Safety Commission (National Police Agency)
総務省	Ministry of Internal Affairs and Communications
法務省	Ministry of Justice
外務省	Ministry of Foreign Affairs
財務省	Ministry of Finance
文部科学省	Ministry of Education, Culture, Sports, Science and Technology
厚生労働省	Ministry of Health, Labour and Welfare
農林水産省	Ministry of Agriculture, Forestry and Fisheries
経済産業省	Ministry of Economy, Trade and Industry
国土交通省	Ministry of Land, Infrastructure, Transport and Tourism
環境省	Ministry of the Environment
防衛省	Ministry of Defense

2 投票、選挙

DL 11_03

vote 投票する、投票、表決
voter 投票者、有権者
voting right, right to vote 投票権
ballot 投票用紙、(1人の)票
hold a referendum on ～について国民(住民)投票をする
elect 選挙で選ぶ
have[hold] an election 選挙を実施する(**election** 選挙)
election day 選挙日
general election 総選挙

USEFUL SENTENCES

今朝早くに投票しました。	I voted early this morning.
日本人は18歳で投票権を得ます。	Japanese have the right to vote at the age of 18.
英国はEU離脱に関する国民投票をしました。	The United Kingdom held a referendum on leaving the EU.
地方自治体の首長は住民により選出されます。	The heads of local governments are elected by the people.
今年の4月に総選挙が実施されます。	The general election will be held in April this year.

run for the Diet
国会議員選挙に立候補する

run for mayor 市長に立候補する
candidate 候補者

go on a campaign, canvass
選挙運動 (遊説) をする

support a candidate 候補者を支持する
election campaign 選挙運動

poll, opinion poll, opinion survey, public opinion poll
世論調査

conduct a (public opinion) poll
世論調査をする

election result
選挙結果

win/lose an election
選挙に勝つ／負ける

USEFUL SENTENCES

その元キャスターは、国会議員選挙に立候補しました。	The former anchor ran for the Diet.
その候補者の家族が選挙運動を行います。	The candidate's family is going on a campaign.
支持している候補者はいますか？	Do you have a candidate to support?
最新の世論調査によると、与党の支持率が少し上昇しました。	According to a recent poll, the ruling party's approval rating has risen slightly.
選挙結果はいつ発表されますか？	When will the election result be announced?
現職が選挙に負けたのですか？	Did the incumbent lose the election?

外交

DL 11_04

diplomacy 外交
diplomat 外交官
foreign policy 外交政策
**Ministry of
Foreign Affairs** 外務省

ally, allied nations 同盟国
make an alliance
同盟を結ぶ

embassy 大使館
ambassador 大使

---

negotiate 交渉する、協議する(**negotiation** 交渉、協議)
intervene 介入する、調停する(**intervention** 介入、調停、仲裁)

USEFUL SENTENCES

外交は、他国と政治的、経済的、文化的関係を
結ぶことです。

Diplomacy is the establishment of political,
economic and cultural relations with other
countries.

私の小さい頃の夢は、外交官でした。

My childhood dream was to be a diplomat.

その国に日本大使館がありますか？

Is there a Japanese Embassy in that country?

sign[form, conclude] a treaty
条約を締結する

sign[conclude] an agreement
合意に署名する

have a summit 首脳会談をする

international organization
国際機構

---

declare 宣言する、公表する（**declaration** 宣言、公表、宣言文）

impose sanctions 制裁を加える

protocol 外交儀礼、儀典

friction 衝突、不和、摩擦

refugee 難民

USEFUL SENTENCES

アヘン戦争終結のため、英国と清は1842年に南京条約を締結しました。

To end the Opium War, the United Kingdom and Qing Dynasty signed the Nanjing Treaty in 1842.

日本とEUは、2018年に経済連携協定を締結しました。

Japan and EU signed an economic partnership agreement (EPA) in 2018.

ポツダム宣言を通して、米国、英国、中国の首脳は日本に降伏を勧告しました。

Through the Potsdam Declaration, the heads of the United States, Britain and China recommended Japan surrender.

社会

Society

妊娠、出産、育児

DL 12_01

妊娠、出産

be pregnant
妊娠している
pregnancy 妊娠
pregnant woman
妊婦

do〔take〕a pregnancy test
妊娠検査をする
pregnancy test kit
妊娠検査キット

have morning sickness
つわりがある

give birth to a baby, deliver a baby
子どもを産む、分娩する
childbirth 出産、分娩

newborn baby
新生児

umbilical cord
へその緒

USEFUL SENTENCES

妊婦さんに席を譲ってください。

できるだけ早く妊娠検査をしてみて。

つわりがひどかったです。

父親が新生児のへその緒を切りました。

Please give seating priority to pregnant women.

Do a pregnancy test as soon as possible.

I had bad morning sickness.

The father cut the umbilical cord of the newborn baby.

due date 出産予定日

deliver[give birth to] ~ by natural birth 自然分娩で産む

have a Caesarean section 帝王切開する

be born by Caesarean section[natural birth] 帝王切開[自然分娩]で産まれる

miscarry, have a miscarriage 流産する

birth rate 出生率

promote[encourage] childbirth 出産を奨励する

pay a childbirth grant 出産奨励金を支給する

impose birth control 産児制限を実施する

USEFUL SENTENCES

一番上の子は自然分娩で産みました。	I delivered my eldest child by natural birth.
姉(妹)は帝王切開で産まれました。	My sister was born by Caesarean section.
政府はさまざまな方法で出産を奨励しています。	The government is encouraging childbirth in a variety of ways.
過去には政府が産児制限を実施しました。	In the past, the government imposed birth control.

帝王切開

「帝王切開」は英語でCaesarean sectionと言いと言います。Caesarean は Caesar（古代ローマの政治家ユリウス・カエサル）の形容詞形です。カエサルがこの方法で産まれたため、Caesarean section という用語が彼の名前に由来しているという説がありますが、これは事実とは異なるそうです。ローマの作家プリニウスが、「切開する」という意味の 'caesum' から 'sectio caesarea' という用語を作ったのですが、caesarea の発音がカエサルと似ていたために生じた誤解だというのです。どうやらそちらの方が正しそうに聞こえますね？

get an abortion 妊娠中絶手術を受ける（**abortion** 堕胎、妊娠中絶）
support abortion 妊娠中絶に賛成する（**pro-choice** 妊娠中絶に賛成の）
oppose abortion 妊娠中絶に反対する（**pro-life** 妊娠中絶に反対の）

postpartum care 産後ケア
postpartum care center 産後ケアセンター
be on maternity leave 出産休暇中だ（**maternity leave** 出産休暇）
be on childcare leave 育児休暇中だ（**childcare leave** 育児休暇）

USEFUL SENTENCES

カトリック教会は妊娠中絶に反対しています。	The Catholic Church opposes abortion.
妊娠中絶に賛成ですか、反対ですか？	Are you pro-choice or pro-life?
最近は大半の母親が産後ケアセンターで産後ケアをします。	Nowadays, most mothers get postpartum care in postpartum care centers.
彼女は今、出産休暇中です。	She is on maternity leave now.
育児休暇はどれだけの長さですか？	How long is your childcare leave?

育児

bring up [raise] a baby

子どもを育てる

breastfeed

母乳で育てる

breastfeeding 母乳育児

bottle feed

育児用ミルクで育てる

bottle feeding

育児用ミルクで育てること

baby bottle 哺乳瓶

change a diaper

おむつを替える

stroller

乳母車、ベビーカー

potty

幼児用便器

baby food

離乳食

childcare facilities

育児施設

daycare center

保育所

nanny, babysitter

ベビーシッター

USEFUL SENTENCES

哺乳瓶をお湯で消毒するのがいいでしょうか？	Would it be good to disinfect the baby bottle with hot water?
おむつを替えたことはありますか？	Have you ever changed a diaper?
うちの子はまだベビーカーに乗りたがります。	My child still wants to ride in a stroller.
子どもに離乳食を手作りしています。	I make my own baby food.
保育所には何歳から行けますか？	At what age can a child go to a daycare center?

2 人権、男女の平等、福祉

`DL 12_03`

protect[support] human rights 人権を保護する［擁護する］
violate[infringe on] human rights 人権を侵害する［踏みにじる］
welfare policy 福祉政策
social worker ソーシャルワーカー

gender equality
男女平等

gender discrimination
性差別

MeToo movement
MeToo運動

welfare 福祉 / **public welfare** 公共の福祉 /
social welfare 社会福祉

USEFUL SENTENCES

現行の捜査方法は、人権を侵害しています。

The current investigation method is infringing on human rights.

男女平等の認識がかなり向上しました。

The perception of gender equality has improved a lot.

MeToo運動は2017年にハリウッドで始まりました。

The MeToo movement started in Hollywood in 2017.

政府はさまざまな公共の福祉政策を実施しています。

The government is implementing various public welfare policies.

welfare for senior citizens[the elderly] 高齢者福祉
aging society 高齢化社会
aged society 高齢社会
basic old-age pension 老齢基礎年金
old-age pensioner 老齢年金受給者

child benefit
児童手当

**support a
single-parent family**
ひとり親家庭を支援する

**welfare for
the disabled
[handicapped]**
障害者福祉

give aid to[relieve] the poor 貧困層を援助する
increase the welfare budget 福祉予算を増やす
universal welfare 普遍的福祉
selective welfare 選択的福祉

高齢化社会、高齢社会、超高齢社会
・aging society: 総人口に占める満65歳以上の割合が7パーセント以上
・aged society: 14パーセント以上
・super-aged society: 21パーセント以上

普遍的福祉、選択的福祉
・universal welfare（普遍的福祉）: 国民のすべてに提供。健康保険、国民年金、学校の給食無償、老齢基礎年金、移動手段、保育費の支援、養育手当など
・selective welfare（選択的福祉）: 必要とする人にだけ提供。生活保護、ひとり親家庭の支援、障害者福祉など

3 災害、事故

災害

natural disaster 自然災害   **human disaster** 人災(人的災害)

fire
火災

forest fire
山火事

earthquake 地震
aftershock 余震

heavy rainfall
暴風雨、豪雨
**localized
heavy rain**
集中豪雨

typhoon
台風

heavy snowfall
大雪

flood
洪水

drought
干ばつ

landslide
山崩れ

tsunami
津波

USEFUL SENTENCES

自然災害は防げなくても、人災は防ぐべきです。

Even if natural disasters cannot be prevented, human disasters should be.

カリフォルニアでは、毎年のように大きな山火事が起こります。

Big forest fires occur almost every year in California.

集中豪雨により山崩れになることがあります。

Localized heavy rain can cause landslides.

今週末、台風が襲来します。

There is a typhoon coming this weekend.

その年は春から夏までひどい干ばつでした。

There was a severe drought from spring to summer that year.

heat wave 猛暑

shelter, refuge 避難所、保護施設、休憩所

cold wave 寒波

evacuee 避難民、被災者

事故

be hit by a car
自動車事故に遭う

have a car crash
車の衝突[追突]事故に遭う

have a fender bender 接触事故に遭う

air crash, (air)plane crash
飛行機墜落事故

suffer shipwreck
海難事故に遭う

survive an accident/a crash/ a shipwreck
事故／衝突・墜落事故／海難事故で生き残る

call an ambulance
救急車を呼ぶ

go to an ER
救急治療室へ行く

be taken to an ER
救急治療室に運ばれていく

USEFUL SENTENCES

地震の被災者たちは避難所に寝泊まりしています。	Evacuees from the earthquake are staying in the shelter.
今日、帰宅途中に接触事故に遭いました。	I had a fender bender on my way home today.
その歌手は飛行機墜落事故で亡くなりました。	The singer died in an airplane crash.
その海難事故で生き残った人たちはPTSDに苦しみました。	Those who survived the shipwreck suffered PTSD.
救急車を呼んでください。	Call an ambulance, please!

4 犯罪

DL 12_05

commit a crime 罪を犯す
violent crime 凶悪犯罪 (殺人、拉致、強盗、性暴力など)
suspect 容疑者
get ~ stolen, be robbed of ~ ～を盗まれる

---

cyber crime
サイバー犯罪
hacker
ハッカー

criminal
犯人、犯罪者

victim
被害者

theft, burglary
窃盗
theif, burglar
窃盗犯

robbery
強盗
robber
強盗犯

**have one's pocket picked,
be[get] pick pocketed**
スリに遭う
pickpocket スリ

con, swindle
詐欺、詐欺を働く
fraud
詐欺、詐欺師

speeding
(車の) スピード違反
speeding ticket
スピード違反キップ

USEFUL SENTENCES

警察は容疑者を指名手配しました。	The police put the suspect on the wanted list.
彼はタブレット PC を盗まれました。	He got his tablet PC stolen.
ローマでスリに遭いました。	I had my pocket picked in Rome.
詐欺に遭ったことがありますか?	Have you ever been swindled?
スピード違反キップを切られました。	I got a speeding ticket.

be〔get〕 hacked

〜をハッキング される

murder

殺人、殺害する

murderer 殺人者
serial murder 連続殺人
serial killer 連続殺人犯

assault, violence

暴行、暴力

arson

放火

arsonist 放火犯
set ~ on fire, set fire to

〜に火をつける［放火する］

kidnap	**sexual violence**	**sexual harassment**	**sexual assault**	**white-collar crime**
誘拐する、拉致する				
kidnapper	性暴力(セクハラ、	セクハラ	性的いやがらせ、	ホワイトカラー犯罪
誘拐犯、拉致犯	性的いやがらせ、		性的暴行	
	性的暴行)			

rape

レイプする、レイプ
(**rapist** レイプ犯)

USEFUL SENTENCES

インスタグラムのアカウントをハッキングされました。	My Instagram account got hacked.
連続殺人犯が20年以上たって捕まりました。	The serial killer was captured after more than 20 years.
彼は暴行の容疑で立件されました。	He was charged with assault.
性暴力を専門に扱う弁護士たちがいます。	There are lawyers who specialize in sexual violence.
ホワイトカラー犯罪は、社会的、経済的、技術的に力を持った人たちが犯します。	White-collar crime is committed by those who have social, economic, or technological power.

bribe
賄賂、賄賂を渡す
bribery 贈収賄

embezzle
横領する

take drugs
麻薬を服用する

drug dealing
麻薬取引

police officer
警察官

patrol car
パトカー

evidence 証拠
clue 手掛かり

fingerprint
指紋

investigate 捜査する
police station 警察署 / **police box** 派出所
prosecutor 検事 / **the prosecution** 検察
investigation technology 捜査技術

USEFUL SENTENCES

その学校長は贈収賄の嫌疑で罷免されました。	The principal of the school was dismissed for bribery charges.
指紋のおかげで犯人を捕まえられました。	They were able to catch the criminal thanks to the fingerprint.
警察がその事件を捜査しています。	The police are investigating the case.
家のすぐ近くに派出所があります。	There's a police box right near my house.
捜査技術が発展し続けています。	Investigation technology continues to develop.

chase
追跡する

flee
逃亡する

arrest
逮捕する

handcuffs
手錠

interrogate 尋問する
interrogation 尋問
confess 自白する

be taken into custody
拘置所に収監される、拘留される

witness 目撃者
request/issue a warrant 令状を要求／発行する
arrest warrant 逮捕令状
search warrant 捜査令状
cold case 未解決事件

USEFUL SENTENCES

男性が現行犯逮捕されました。	A man was arrested at the scene of the crime.
検事は容疑者が自白したと言いました。	The prosecutor said that the suspect had confessed.
その男性は結局、拘留されました。	The man was eventually taken into custody.
事件の目撃者として警察署に行きました。	I went to the police station as a witness in the case.
裁判所は令状を発行しました。	The court issued a warrant.
未解決事件の解決に努めている警察官たちがいます。	There are police officers who are trying to solve the cold cases.

DL 12_07

abide by[keep, obey, observe] the law 法を守る
apply the law 法を適用する、法を施行する
court 法廷
try 裁判をする / **trial** 裁判
case 事件
file a lawsuit[suit] 訴訟を起こす (**lawsuit** 訴訟、告訴)
accuse 告発する、告訴する
indict, charge 起訴する
lawyer 弁護士
prosecutor 検察官、検事

USEFUL SENTENCES

大半の人は法を守ります。	Most people abide by the law.
すべての人たちに対し、法は等しく適用されるべきです。	The law should be applied equally to everyone.
その男性は殺人で裁判にかけられました。	The man was tried for murder.
彼女は夫を相手に訴訟を起こしました。	She filed a lawsuit against her husband.
市民団体がその政治家を告発しました。	A civic group accused the politician.
弁護士を雇うのに多額のお金がかかりますか？	Does it cost a lot of money to hire a lawyer?

judge
裁判官、判事、
裁判する

**defendant,
the accused**
被告

plaintiff
原告

juror
陪審員

jury
陪審員団

rule
判決を下す

ruling, decision
判決

witness (法廷の)証人
give testimony (法廷で)証言する
plead, defend 弁論する
dismiss 棄却する

USEFUL SENTENCES

裁判官は検察官に警告しました。	The judge warned the prosecutor.
被告は法廷に出廷しませんでした。	The defendant did not appear in court.
刑事事件の原告は検察官です。	The plaintiff in a criminal case is the prosecutor.
裁判官が被告無罪の判決を下しました。	The judge ruled the defendant not guilty.
彼が裁判に出廷して証言をしました。	He attended the trial and gave testimony.

sentence 判決を下す、判決

be sentenced to ~ ～の刑を受ける

final trial 確定判決

be found guilty 有罪判決を受ける

be found not guilty 無罪判決を受ける

fine, impose a fine 罰金を課す（**fine** 罰金）

appeal 控訴する

serve ~ in prison ～服役する

go to jail[prison], be sent to[put into] jail[prison] 刑務所に行く

USEFUL SENTENCES

裁判所はその被告に無期懲役の判決を下しました。	The court sentenced the defendant to life imprisonment.
その連続殺人犯は死刑を宣告されました。	The serial killer was sentenced to death.
警察は彼に罰金10万円を課しました。	The police fined him 100,000 yen.
検察官は直ちに控訴しました。	The prosecutor appealed immediately.
彼は17年間服役しました。	He served 17 years in prison.

法廷の種類
Supreme Court 最高裁判所
High Court 高等裁判所
District[Local] Court 地方裁判所
Family Court 家庭裁判所

裁判
第一審 : the first trial
第二審（控訴審）: the second trial
第三審（上告審）: the third trial, the final trial

Even if natural disasters cannot be prevented,

HUMAN DISASTERS SHOULD BE.

6 メディア、言論

`DL 12_09`

the media メディア（**the mass media** マスメディア）
journalism ジャーナリズム
news agency 通信社
article 記事
editorial 社説
cover 取材する
correspondent 特派員
breaking news ニュース速報、特報

---

the press
マスコミ、報道陣

morning/evening (news)paper
朝刊／夕刊

online news website
オンラインのニュースサイト

journalist, reporter
記者

USEFUL SENTENCES

通信社は新聞社と放送局にニュースを提供します。 — The news agency provides news to newspapers and broadcasters.

最近は、大半の人がインターネットでニュース記事を読みます。 — Nowadays, most people read news articles on the internet.

彼女の父親は中国特派員でした。 — Her father was a correspondent in China.

その裁判の結果がテレビのニュース速報で流れます。 — The result of the trial is coming out in breaking news on TV.

マスコミの役割と責任について考える必要があります。 — We need to think about the role and responsibility of the press.

その記者は、その事件を何年も取材しています。 — The journalist has been covering the case for years.

have an interview インタビューをする
give an interview インタビューに応じる
interviewer インタビュアー（インタビューする人）
interviewee インタビュイー（インタビューされる人）

broadcast 放送、放送する
broadcaster, broadcasting station
[**company**] 放送局、放送会社
TV/radio station テレビ／ラジオ局
internet broadcast インターネット放送
live broadcast 生放送

give[hold] a press conference 記者会見をする（**press conference** 記者会見）
weekly/monthly magazine 週刊／月刊誌
personal broadcasting 個人放送

USEFUL SENTENCES

昨日、テレビ局のインタビューに応じました。	I gave an interview to a TV station yesterday.
そのコンサートがテレビで放送されました。	The concert was broadcast on TV.
姉は放送局でラジオのプロデューサーとして働いています。	My sister works as a radio producer at a broadcasting station.
その歌手が引退記者会見をしました。	The singer gave a press conference about his retirement.
最近は多くの人が個人放送をしています。	There are a lot of people doing personal broadcasting these days.

believe in ～を信じる
religion 宗教

convert to ～に改宗する
faith 信仰・信教

Christianity キリスト教
Christian キリスト教徒
Catholic Church カトリック教会
Catholic カトリック教徒
Catholicism カトリシズム
Protestantism
プロテスタンティズム
Protestant プロテスタント

Buddhism 仏教
Buddhist 仏教徒

Islam
イスラム教

Muslim
イスラム教徒

Hinduism ヒンドゥー教,
Hindu ヒンドゥー教徒

Judaism ユダヤ教,
Judaist, Jew ユダヤ教徒

* **shamanism** シャーマニズム
* **Confucianism** 儒教
* **Taoism** 道教

USEFUL SENTENCES

彼は結婚後、カトリックに改宗しました。 He converted to Catholicism after he got married.

カトリック教会、プロテスタンティズムの
どちらもキリスト教に属します。 Both the Catholic Church and Protestantism
belong to Christianity.

イスラム教徒は豚肉を食べません。 Muslims do not eat pork.

ユダヤ教は新約聖書を認めていません。 Judaism does not recognize the New Testament.

Bible
(キリスト教・
ユダヤ教の)聖書

* **Buddhist scriptures**
仏教の経典

go to mass
ミサに参列する

attend a service
礼拝に参加する

be baptized
洗礼を受ける

baptism 洗礼

attend/hold a Buddhist service
法事に参加する／を行う

cathedral
大聖堂(司教のいる聖堂)

church
教会

Buddhist temple
寺、仏教寺院

mosque
イスラム寺院

synagogue
ユダヤ教の礼拝堂

USEFUL SENTENCES

祖母は仏教の経典をよく読んでいます。	My grandmother often reads Buddhist scriptures.
その家族は日曜日になるとミサに参列します。	The family goes to mass every Sunday.
水曜日にも礼拝に参加するのですか？	Do you attend the service on Wednesdays as well?
10年前にカトリックの洗礼を受けました。	I was baptized a Catholic 10 years ago.
東京にはイスラム寺院があります。	There is a mosque in Tokyo.

DL 12_11

cross
十字架

pray 祈る
prayer 祈り

preach
説教する

hymn
聖歌、讃美歌

the Pope
ローマ教皇

cardinal
枢機卿

priest
司祭、神父

nun
修道女

minister
牧師

(Buddhist) monk
僧侶

Buddhist nun 尼僧

rabbi
ラビ
（ユダヤ教の律法学者）

imam
イマーム、
イスラム教の指導者

USEFUL SENTENCES

母は毎日、朝と晩にお祈りをします。

My mom prays every morning and evening.

子どものころ教わった讃美歌のうち、覚えているものが何曲かあります。

I remember a few of the hymns I learned as a child.

ローマ教皇は全世界のカトリック教会の長です。

The Pope is the head of the Catholic Church around the world.

おじはカトリックの神父です。

My uncle is a Catholic priest.

Nowadays, most people read news articles on the internet.

There are a lot of people doing personal broadcasting these days.

LIVE STREAMING

13

交通、運転

Traffic & Driving

交通全般

**drive a car/
truck/van**

自動車／トラック／ワゴン車
を運転する

**take a bus/taxi/
train/subway/tram/
boat/ship/ferry**

バス／タクシー／電車／地下鉄／
路面電車／ボート／船／
フェリーに乗る

**ride a bike[bicycle]/
motorbike[motorcycle]/
scooter/moped/horse**

自転車／オートバイ／
スクーター／モペッド／
馬に乗る

get on/off a bus バスに乗る／から降りる

get in/out of a car/taxi 自動車／タクシーに乗る／から降りる

catch a train/bus 電車／バスに乗る、電車／バスに間に合う

miss a train/bus 電車／バスに乗り遅れる

give someone a ride ～を車に乗せてあげる

hitchhike ヒッチハイクをする

USEFUL SENTENCES

今日市内に出るため、地下鉄に乗りました。

包みを抱えたおばあさんが苦労してバスに
乗り込みました。

危うく電車に乗り遅れるところでした。

友達が家まで車に乗せてくれました。

I took the subway to go downtown today.

An old lady with a bundle got on the bus with
difficulty.

I almost missed the train.

My friend gave me a ride home.

英語の道路標識
STOP: 停止
DEAD END: 行き止まり
ONE WAY: 一方通行
DO NOT ENTER: 進入禁止

passenger
乗客

driver
運転者

pedestrian
歩行者

road〔traffic〕sign
道路標識、交通標識

traffic signal〔light〕 信号機
（**red light** 赤信号
yellow light 黄信号
green light 青信号）

bus stop
バス停留所

taxi stand
タクシー乗り場

train station 鉄道駅
platform
プラットホーム、（電車やバスなどの）乗降口

ticket office
切符売り場

get through the ticket gate〔ticket barrier〕
改札口を通る

USEFUL SENTENCES

車両よりも歩行者が優先されるべきです。	Pedestrians should be given priority over vehicles.
時々、道路標識を理解しにくいことがあります。	Sometimes it's hard to understand the road signs.
信号を守らない運転者が何人かいます。	There are a few drivers that don't observe traffic signals.
病院の前にタクシー乗り場があります。	There's a taxi stand in front of the hospital.
電車がプラットホームを離れたところです。	The train has just left the platform.
改札口を出るとすぐにコンビニが見えるでしょう。	You'll see the convenience store as soon as you get through the ticket gate.

**fasten〔wear〕
a seat belt**
シートベルトを締める

go straight
直進する

turn left/right
左折／右折する

change lanes
車線変更する

park
駐車する

parking lot
駐車場

---

speed up, accelerate 加速する

slow down 減速する

brake ブレーキをかける、ブレーキを踏む

turn on a turn signal, put a turn signal on ウインカーを出す

pick someone up 〜を乗せる

drop someone off 〜を降ろす

observe/neglect/violate a traffic signal 信号を守る／無視する／に違反する

honk one's horn クラクションを鳴らす

USEFUL SENTENCES

今は車のどの席でもシートベルトを締める必要があります。	Now we need to fasten our seat belts on every seat of the vehicle.
車を運転するなら、駐車場がない所へは行けないですね。	If you drive, you won't be able to go to places without a parking lot.
坂を下るときは減速すべきです。	You should slow down when you're going downhill.
急ブレーキをかけるべきではありません。	You shouldn't suddenly brake.
ウインカーを出さずに車線変更する車がいます。	There are cars that change lanes without turning on their turn signals.
必要なくクラクションを鳴らすのは望ましくありません。	It's not desirable to honk your horn unless it's necessary.

have a car accident[crash]
自動車事故を起こす

break down
故障する

have a flat tire
タイヤがパンクする

tow a car
車をけん引する

have[get] the car checked/ repaired
車を点検／修理してもらう

car service center カーセンター
auto[car] repair shop 自動車修理店
mechanic 整備士

gas station
ガソリンスタンド

put gas in a car 車にガソリンを入れる
fill a car with gas, gas up ガソリンを満タンにする
(gasoline ガソリン **, diesel** 軽油 **)**

EV charging station
(electric vehicle charging station)
電気自動車の充電スタンド

charge an electric car
電気自動車に充電する

USEFUL SENTENCES

運転を始めてから、自動車事故を起こしたことはありませんか？	Haven't you ever had a car accident since you started driving?
車が故障して、直してもらうのに多額の費用がかかりました。	My car broke down and it cost me a lot to have it repaired.
カーセンターで車の点検を受けました。	I had my car checked at the car service center.
いちばん近いガソリンスタンドはどこ？	Where is the nearest gas station?
車にガソリンを入れてから出発しましょう。	Let's put gas in the car before we hit the road.
近くに電気自動車の充電スタンドがありますか？	Is there an EV charging station nearby?

`DL 13_03`

wash a car
洗車する

car wash
洗車(場)

go through an automatic car wash
自動洗車をする、
自動洗車機を通る

speed limit
制限速度、速度制限

speed camera
スピード違反
取り締まりカメラ

get a speeding/ parking ticket
スピード／駐車違反の
キップを切られる

be congested 渋滞している
be stuck in a traffic jam
交通渋滞に巻き込まれる

centerline
センターライン

crosswalk 横断歩道

get one's driver's license
運転免許を取る

used car 中古車

take out car insurance 自動車保険に入る

USEFUL SENTENCES

ガソリンスタンドでガソリンを入れた後、自動洗車をしました。	I put the gas in at the gas station and went through an automatic car wash.
その高速道路の制限速度は時速100キロメートルです。	The speed limit on the highway is 100 kilometers per hour.
今月だけで、駐車違反のキップを2回切られました。	I got two parking tickets this month alone.
その道はひどく渋滞していました。実は、そこはいつも渋滞がひどいのです。	The road was very congested. In fact, there is always a heavy traffic jam on that road.
何歳で運転免許を取りましたか？	At what age did you get your driver's license?
中古車を買うときに気を付けるべき点は何ですか？	What should I be careful about when I buy a used car?

車の構造：外部

trunk トランク, trunk lid トランクの蓋

sunroof サンルーフ

wiper ワイパー

windshield, windscreen フロントガラス

bonnet, hood ボンネット、フード

side mirror サイドミラー

head lamp[light] ヘッドライト

front bumper フロントバンパー

fog lamp フォグランプ

radiator grille ラジエータグリル

door ドア

front wheel 前輪

rear wheel 後輪

hubcab ホイールキャップ

brake light ブレーキランプ

rear bumper リアバンパー

fender フェンダー、泥よけ

gas tank door 給油口,
gas tank cap 給油口カバー

車の構造：内部

dashboard ダッシュボード

steering wheel ハンドル

rearview mirror バックミラー

ventilator 通風孔

horn クラクション

GPS navigation system[device] ナビゲーション

brake ブレーキ

accelerator アクセル

3 道を探す、方向

DL 13_04

direction 方向
signpost 標識、道しるべ
road map 道路地図
compass 羅針盤
northeast 北東
northwest 北西
southeast 南東
southwest 南西
street (両側に建物が並ぶ)道路 (**st.**)
avenue 大通り (**ave.**)
boulevard 街路樹がある大通り (**blvd.**)
road (車が走る)道路

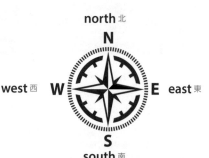

USEFUL SENTENCES

最近はGPSがあるので、道路地図を持ち歩く人は
ほどんどいません。

Nowadays, few people carry road maps
because there are GPS navigation systems.

> **boulevard, street, avenue, road**
> • boulevard: 両側に街路樹のある広い道路。普通は中央分離帯がある。
> • street: 両側に建物のある道。普通は東西をつなぐ道路で、avenueと垂直に交わる。
> • avenue: 両側に建物のある道。普通は南北をつなぐ道路で、streetと垂直に交わる。
> • road: 2つの地点をつなぐ、主に車が走る道。

intersection, junction, crossroads
交差点、四差路

highway
幹線道路
freeway, expressway
高速道路

one-way street
一方通行の道

turn left/right
左折／右折する

shoulder 路肩
sidewalk, pavement, footpath 歩道
go straight (**ahead**) 直進する、まっすぐ進む
go past 〜を通り過ぎる
stop at/in front of 〜で／の前で止まる
take the first/second right/left 1つ目／2つ目の分かれ道で右／左に行く
read a map 地図を見る
ask the way (**to** 〜に行く) 道を尋ねる/**ask for directions** 道を尋ねる

USEFUL SENTENCES

その交差点で右折してください。	Turn right at the intersection.
高速道路は徐行できません。	You can't drive slow on the expressway.
200メートルくらい直進して左折してください。	Go straight for about 200 meters and then turn left.
路肩を走行するのは危険です。	It's dangerous to drive on the shoulder.
郵便局を過ぎて地下鉄の駅の所で止めてください。	Go past the post office and stop at the subway station.
分からなければ人に道を聞いてください。	Ask people the way if you don't know.

CHAPTER

14

スマートフォン、インターネット、SNS

Smartphone, Internet, Social Media

スマートフォン

DL 14_01

**unlock
the smartphone**
スマートフォンのロックを
解除する

text message
テキストメッセージ

text
テキストメッセージを送る

messaging[texting] app
メッセンジャーアプリ
（ラインなど）

---

slide to unlock, unlock the phone by sliding it to the side
スライドしてスマートフォンのロックを解除する

enter a password/pattern to unlock the phone
パスワード／パターンを入力してスマートフォンのロックを解除する

make a (phone) call 電話をかける

answer[get] a (phone) call, answer the phone 電話に出る

make[do] a video call ビデオ通話をする

use one's smartphone to access the internet[to get online]
スマートフォンでインターネットに接続する

USEFUL SENTENCES

彼女は一日中テキストメッセージを送っているようです。	She seems to be texting all day.
パターンを入力してスマートフォンのロックを解除する。	I enter a pattern to unlock my smartphone.
彼女は電話に出ないことがよくあります。	She often doesn't answer the phone.
彼はよく幼い娘とビデオ通話をしています。	He often makes video calls with his young daughter.
最近は多くの人たちがスマートフォンでインターネットに接続します。	Nowadays, many people use their smartphones to access the internet.

use an app[application] アプリを使用する
download an app[application]
アプリをダウンロードする

install an app[application]
アプリをインストールする

update an app[application]
アプリをアップデートする

a battery runs out
バッテリーが切れる

〈high-speed〉〈battery〉charger (高速)充電器
portable charger ポータブル充電器
home screen ホーム画面
lock screen ロック画面

charge a phone
電話[スマホ]を充電する

USEFUL SENTENCES

そのラジオアプリをインストールした？	Did you install that radio app?
アップデートする必要のあるアプリが5つある。	There are five apps that need to be updated.
バッテリーが切れるから充電してまた電話します。	The battery has run out so I'm going to charge it and call you again.
高速充電器でスマートフォンを充電するといいですよ。	It's good to charge your smartphone with a high-speed charger.
スマートフォンのバッテリーがすぐに切れるので、ポータブル充電器を持ち歩かなければなりません。	The smartphone battery runs out quickly, so I have to carry around a portable charger.
ホーム画面をうちの犬の写真にしました。	I put a picture of my dog on my smartphone home screen.

2 インターネット、メール

`DL 14_02`

インターネット

access a website
ウェブサイトに接続する

surf[browse] the internet
インターネットをざっと見て回る

****

enter one's user ID and password
ユーザーIDとパスワードを入力する

bookmark a website[page]
ウェブサイトを
ブックマーク登録する
bookmark ブックマーク

shop online
インターネット[オンライン]ショッピング
をする
internet[online] shopping
インターネット[オンライン]ショッピング

click
クリックする

look[search] for information on a web portal ポータルサイトで情報を検索する
sign in[log in to] a website ウェブサイトにログインする
sign out of[log out of] a website ウェブサイトからログアウトする
copy コピーする
paste 貼り付ける

USEFUL SENTENCES

1日に1時間前後、ネットサーフィンをしていると思います。	I think I spend about an hour a day surfing the internet.
ログインするにはユーザーIDとパスワードを入力してください。	Please enter your user ID and password to sign in.
そのウェブサイトをブックマーク登録しました。	I bookmarked that website.
インターネットショッピングをよくします。	I often shop online.
この頃は皆、ポータルサイトで情報を探したり、ニュースを見たりしています。	These days, people look for information and watch the news on web portals.
その文をコピーして貼り付けてもいいです。	You can copy and paste the sentence.

Eメール

sender 送信者

inbox 受信トレイ

recipient 宛先

subject 件名

outbox 送信トレイ, sent email 送信済みメール

drafts 下書き

body 本文

spam[junk] email 迷惑メール

trash ごみ箱

deleted items 削除済みアイテム

attachment 添付ファイル

send an email メールを送る

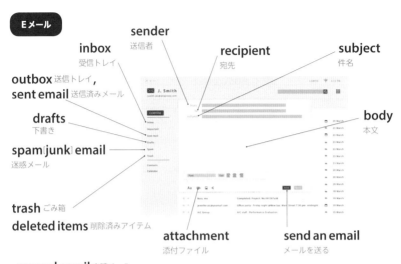

* unread email 未読メール
* CC(carbon copy) CC（で送る）

create an email account メールアカウントを作る
log on[in] to one's email account メールアカウントにログインする
write an email メールを書く
reply to an email メールに返信する
forward an email メールを転送する

USEFUL SENTENCES

件名を書かずに彼女にメールを送ってしまいました。 I sent her an email without a subject.
受信トレイに未読メールが50件以上あります。 I have over 50 unread mails in my mailbox.
新しいメールアカウントを作りました。 I've created a new email account.
返信しなければならないメールが10件以上あります。 I have over 10 emails to reply to.
そのメールを私に転送してください。 Please forward the email to me.

3 ソーシャルメディア、SNS

blog ブログ、ブログに投稿する
blogger ブロガー
write[put] a post on a blog ブログに投稿する
blog post, post ブログ記事、投稿

Twitter user ツイッター利用者
Twitter feed ツイッターのフィード
tweet ツイートする、ツイートされたメッセージ

Instagram feed インスタグラムのフィード
Instagrammer インスタグラムの利用者
Instagrammable インスタ映えする

follow somebody on Twitter/Instagram
ツイッター／インスタグラムで～をフォローする
follower フォロワー／ **following** フォロー

USEFUL SENTENCES

しばらくブログに投稿していません。	It's been a while since I wrote a post on my blog.
このツイート見て。	Look at this tweet.
彼のインスタグラムのフィードを見ていたら時間がたつのも忘れました。	I've lost track of time watching his Instagram feed.
そこは東京でインスタ映えする10大スポットのひとつです。	It is one of the 10 most Instagrammable spots in Tokyo.
ツイッターでその作家をフォローしました。	I followed the writer on Twitter.
その歌手は100万人を超えるフォロワーがいます。	The singer has over a million followers.

have a Facebook account
フェイスブックのアカウントを持っている

join Facebook フェイスブックに登録する

write[put] a post on Facebook フェイスブックに投稿する

YouTube creator, YouTuber
YouTube クリエイター、ユーチューバー

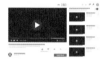

open a YouTube channel YouTube チャンネルを開設する

upload[post] a video on YouTube
YouTube に動画をアップする

subscribe to a YouTube channel
YouTube チャンネルを登録する

watch[view] a YouTube video YouTube 動画を見る

press "like"
「いいね」を押す

write a comment
コメントを書き込む

block someone
〜をブロックする

troll
悪質コメントを書き込む、コメント荒らしをする人

USEFUL SENTENCES

フェイスブックのアカウントは持っているけど、ほとんど使いません。	I have a Facebook account, but I rarely use it.
猫22匹を飼っている人のYouTube チャンネルを登録して見ています。	I'm subscribing to the YouTube channel of a person who has 22 cats.
寝る前にYouTube動画を何本か見るのが習慣です。	It's my habit to watch some YouTube videos before going to bed.
彼は私の投稿に「いいね」を押しました。	He pressed "like" on my post.
ほとんどコメントを書き込みません。	I hardly ever write any comments.
そのボーイバンドは、悪質コメントを書き込む人たちを訴えました。	The boy band sued trolls.

15

教育

Education

1 教育全般

DL 15_01

kindergarten
幼稚園

elementary school
小学校

middle school
中学校

high school
高校

college
大学(学士号取得までが可能)、単科大学

university
総合大学

semester 学期	**coeducational** (**coed**) 男女共学の
graduate school 大学院	**major** 専攻、～を専攻する(**major in ~**)
academy, technical school 専門学校	**cram school** 予備校、塾

USEFUL SENTENCES

私が子どものときは、幼稚園に通う子は少数でした。	When I was a kid, only a few children went to kindergarten.
私が通っていた高校は男女共学でした。	My high school was coeducational.
私は大学で心理学を専攻しました。	I majored in psychology in university.
多くの中学生たちが、塾に通っています。	Many middle school students attend cram schools.

lecture 講義
lecture room 講義室

textbook
教科書

diploma
卒業証書、修了証

library
図書館

laboratory
実験室、実習室、練習室

dormitory
寄宿舎

credit 単位

degree 学位

essay 課題（エッセー、リポート）

thesis 論文

midterm exam 中間試験

final exam 期末試験

USEFUL SENTENCES

そこに応募するには4年制大学の卒業証書が必要です。	I need a university diploma to apply for it.
その学部の学生たちは実験室で夜遅くまで実験と研究をしています。	The department's students experiment and study until late at night in the laboratory.
大学に行ったら寄宿舎で生活することを希望していました。	I hoped I'd live in a dormitory when I'd go to college.
今学期は何単位取る予定ですか？	How many credits are you taking this semester?
週末はリポートを書くので忙しかったです。	I've been busy writing an essay over the weekend.
来週は期末試験ですね。	Next week, we're taking the final exam.

professor
教授
instructor
大学の専任講師、
(特定の技術やスポーツの)講師、指導者

graduate
大学卒業者、卒業生

lifelong learning
生涯学習、生涯教育
online learning
オンライン学習

freshman (高校、大学の)新入生、1年生
sophomore (高校、大学の)2年生
junior (4年制大学の)3年生
senior (高校、大学の)最上級生
undergraduate 大学の学部生
bachelor's degree 学士号
master's degree 修士号
doctoral[doctor's] degree, doctorate, Ph. D. 博士号

USEFUL SENTENCES

「生涯学習」という言葉を知らないのですか？
何歳でも学べるのですよ。

Don't you know the phrase "lifelong learning"?
You can learn at any age.

私は大学2年生のとき、英国文学史を学びました。

I studied the history of English literature in my
sophomore year.

彼女は学部生で、彼氏は大学院生です。

She is an undergraduate and her boyfriend is a
graduate school student.

教授として任用されるためには博士号が
必要です。

You need a doctor's degree to be hired as a
professor.

アメリカ、カナダ、韓国などの大学教授システム
lecturer 非常勤講師 〉instructor 専任講師 〉assistant professor 助教 〉
associate professor 准教授 〉professor 教授、正教授(full professor)

attend a class
授業に出る、受講する

**take[sit]
an exam[a test]**
試験を受ける

**pass/fail
an exam**
試験に受かる／落ちる

graduate from
〜を卒業する

get a degree
学位を得る

enter 〜に入学する

enroll in (大学など) に入る、(授業) に履修登録する

take[listen to] a course[class] 講義 [授業] を受ける

earn credits 単位を取得する

get an A A を取る / **get a good grade** 良い成績を取る

apply for/get a scholarship 奨学金を申請する／受け取る

take a year off (**from school**) 1 年休学する

USEFUL SENTENCES

今週は毎日試験があります。	I'm taking tests every day this week.
今学期、西洋哲学の受講を申請しました。	I enrolled in Western philosophy class this semester.
毎週、詩の授業を受けています。	I'm taking a poetry class every week.
卒業するため、今学期20単位取る必要がありますよ。	You need to earn 20 credits this semester to graduate.
大学を1年休学しました。	I took a year off from college.

中学・高校

art 美術

biology 生物

chemistry 化学

English 英語

ethics 道徳、倫理

geography 地理

home economics 家庭科

Japanese history 日本史

Japanese language 国語

math, mathematics 数学

music 音楽

PE(**physical education**) 体育

physics 物理

science 科学

second foreign language 第2外国語

social studies 社会

world history 世界史

大学

aesthetics 美学

agriculture 農学

anthropology 人類学

archaeology 考古学

architecture 建築学

astronomy 天文学

biology 生物学

business studies, business administration 経営学

ceramics 陶磁工芸

chemical engineering 化学工学

chemistry 化学

communication コミュニケーション学

dentistry 歯学

drama 演劇

economics 経済学
education 教育学
electrical engineering 電子工学
English education 英語教育
fashion design 衣装デザイン
geography 地理学
geology 地質学
history 歴史学
industrial design 産業デザイン、工業デザイン
industrial engineering 産業工学
international relations 国際関係論
Japanese literature 国文学
journalism and broadcasting 新聞放送学
law 法学
literature 文学
math, mathematics 数学
mechanical engineering 機械工学
media and communication メディアコミュニケーション学
medicine 医学
microbiology 微生物学
nursing science 看護学
oriental medicine 漢方医学
painting 絵画
philosophy 哲学
physics 物理学
political science 政治学
psychology 心理学
sculpture 彫刻
sociology 社会学
veterinary medicine 獣医学

DL 15_04

speak
(言語を)話す

practice
(言語を)練習する

be fluent in
(言語が)流ちょうである

speak ~ fluently
(言語を)流ちょうに話す

go to an English conversation school
英会話教室に通う

learn/practice English conversation
英会話を習う／練習する

bilingual
バイリンガルの

multilingual
マルチリンガルの

(言語が) is poor 下手な
be good/poor at ～がうまい／下手な
get rusty さびつく、下手になる
native speaker ネイティブスピーカー
speaking/listening/reading/writing skills
スピーキング／リスニング／リーディング／ライティングの技能

USEFUL SENTENCES

中国語を話せますか？ — Can you speak Chinese?

彼は英語とドイツ語が流ちょうです。 — He is fluent in English and German.

塾で英会話を習いました。 — I learned English conversation at the academy.

英語が下手で申し訳ございません。 — I'm sorry my English is poor.

彼女はネイティブスピーカーのように英語を話す。 — She speaks English like a native speaker.

どうすれば英語ライティングの技能を向上できるでしょうか？ — How can I improve my English writing skills?

language barrier
言葉の壁

vocabulary
語彙

grammar
文法

translate 翻訳する
translation 翻訳
translator 翻訳家

interpret 通訳する
interpretation 通訳

interpreter 通訳者
simultaneous interpreter
同時通訳者

accent アクセント、なまり
intonation イントネーション
pronunciation 発音 (**pronounce** 発音する)

USEFUL SENTENCES

彼女は英語の語彙が豊富だ。	She has a large English vocabulary.
私は英語で意思疎通をすることはできますが、文法は弱いです。	I can communicate in English, but my English grammar is weak.
私の子どもの夢は同時通訳者になることです。	My child's dream is to become a simultaneous interpreter.
彼はインドなまりの英語を話す。	He speaks English with an Indian accent.
その単語は発音が難しいです。	It's hard to pronounce that word.

世界、環境

World & Environment

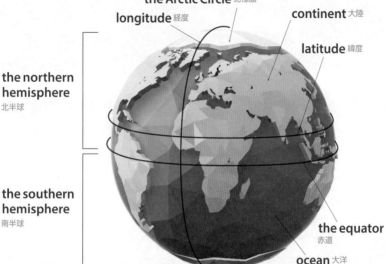

the North Pole 北極 / the Arctic 北極、北極地方
the Arctic Circle 北極圏

longitude 経度

continent 大陸

latitude 緯度

the northern
hemisphere
北半球

the southern
hemisphere
南半球

the equator
赤道

ocean 大洋

the South Pole 南極 / the Antarctic 南極、南極地方
the Antarctic Circle 南極圏 / Antarctica 南極大陸

(the) Earth, (the) planet earth 地球

USEFUL SENTENCES

アイスランドは北極圏のすぐ南側に位置しています。	Iceland is located just south of the Arctic Circle.
東京は北緯35.7度、東経139.7度に位置しています。	Tokyo is located at 35.7 degrees north latitude and 139.7 degrees east longitude.
南半球では夏にクリスマスを祝います。	They celebrate Christmas during the summer in the southern hemisphere.
エクアドルは赤道の上にあるため、そのような名前が付けられました。	Ecuador got its name because it lies on the equator.
地球は太陽系に属する惑星です。	The Earth is a planet in the solar system.

the Arctic Ocean
北極海

Eurasia ユーラシア

Europe ヨーロッパ

North America
北アメリカ

Asia アジア

the Atlantic Ocean
大西洋

the Atlantic Ocean
大西洋

Africa アフリカ

the Pacific Ocean 太平洋

the Southern Ocean, the Antarctic Ocean
南極海

Australia/Oceania
オーストラリア／オセアニア

the Indian Ocean
インド洋

South America
南アメリカ

Antarctica
南極大陸

USEFUL SENTENCES

最も大きな大陸はユーラシアで、2番目に大きいのはアフリカです。	The largest continent is Eurasia and the second largest is Africa.
地球で最も広い海は太平洋です。	The largest ocean on Earth is the Pacific Ocean.
南極海は、南極大陸を取り囲んでいる海を指します。	The Antarctic Ocean refers to the ocean surrounding Antarctica.

UNIT 2 地形、地理

`DL 16_02`

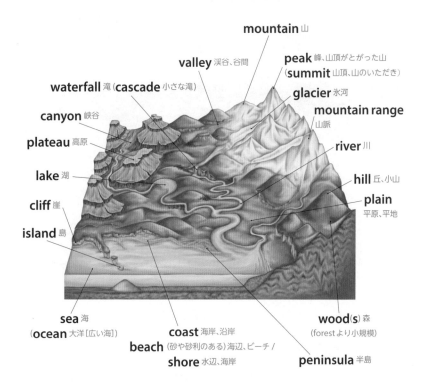

mountain 山
valley 渓谷、谷間
peak 峰、山頂がとがった山（**summit** 山頂、山のいただき）
waterfall 滝（**cascade** 小さな滝）
glacier 氷河
canyon 峡谷
mountain range 山脈
plateau 高原
river 川
lake 湖
hill 丘、小山
cliff 崖
plain 平原、平地
island 島
sea 海（**ocean** 大洋[広い海]）
coast 海岸、沿岸
beach （砂や砂利のある）海辺、ビーチ / **shore** 水辺、海岸
wood(s) 森（forestより小規模）
peninsula 半島

USEFUL SENTENCES

年を取るにつれ、海より山が好きになりました。 As I get older, I like mountains better than the sea.

その山脈が、中部地方と南部地方とを隔てています。 The mountain range borders the central and southern regions.

地球温暖化により、毎年多くの氷河が溶けてなくなっています。 Due to global warming, lots of glaciers are melting away each year.

私の家の裏に丘があります。 There is a hill behind my house.

シンガポールはマレー半島の南端に位置しています。 Singapore is located at the southern tip of the Malay Peninsula.

リオデジャネイロのコパカバーナビーチは、世界で最も有名な海岸の一つです。 Copacabana Beach in Rio de Janeiro is one of the world's most famous beaches.

干潮時、その島は陸地とつながり、その間を歩くことができます。 At low tide, the island is connected to the land and you can walk between.

世界で最も広くて高い高原はチベット高原で、しばしば世界の屋根と呼ばれます。 The largest and highest plateau in the world is the Tibetan Plateau, often called the roof of the world.

beach, coast, shore
- beach: 人々が海水浴をしに行って日光浴をする、砂や砂利のある海辺や湖畔
- coast: 海辺やその周りの地帯
- shore: 湖や海の岸

volcano 火山 **cave** 洞窟 **desert** 砂漠 **dune** 砂丘

forest 森、森林 **rain forest** 雨林 **jungle** 密林
swamp 沼 **iceberg** 氷山 **stream** 谷川、小川
pond 池 **grassland, meadow, pasture** 草むら、草原
field 野原、畑 **farmland** 農地 **countryside** 田舎、田園地帯
wave 波 **horizon** 水平線、地平線
rising tide, high tide, flood tide 満ち潮、満潮 **low tide** 引き潮、干潮

USEFUL SENTENCES

世界で最も広い高温砂漠はアフリカのサハラ砂漠です。	The largest hot desert in the world is the Sahara in Africa.
アマゾンの雨林は世界最大の熱帯雨林です。	The Amazon rain forest is the largest tropical rain forest in the world.
羊の群れが草原で草を食べています。	A flock of sheep is grazing in the meadow.
風があまりないので波が穏やかです。	Since there's not much wind, the waves are calm.
遠くの地平線に太陽がかかっています。	There's the sun on the horizon far away.

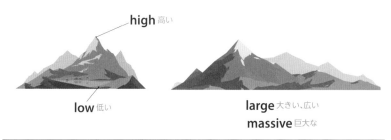

high 高い

low 低い

large 大きい、広い
massive 巨大な

wide 広い　　narrow 狭い

shallow 浅い　　deep 深い

steep 険しい、切り立った
sharp 険しい、急勾配の

vast, extensive 広々とした、広大な

USEFUL SENTENCES

カスピ海は世界で最も大きな湖です。　The Caspian Sea is the largest lake in the world.

オーストラリア中部にあるウルルは、巨大な一枚岩です。　Uluru, in central Australia, is a massive rock.

アマゾンは世界でいちばん広い川ですか？　Is the Amazon River the widest river in the world?

子どもたちは浅い小川で遊んでいます。　The children are playing in a shallow stream.

彼は険しい岩壁をロープ1本で登っていました。　He was climbing up a steep rock with a rope.

その家族は広大な土地を所有していました。　The family owned a vast tract of land.

259

3 自然、物質

DL 16_04

nature 自然 (**Mother Nature** 大自然)
creature 生物、生命体
microorganism 微生物　　**plant** 植物

ecosystem 生態系
organism 有機体、(小さい) 生物
animal 動物

動物

mammal
哺乳類

bird
鳥類

amphibian
両生類

reptile
は虫類

fish
魚類

insect, bug
昆虫

USEFUL SENTENCES

それは生態系の秩序を破壊します。	It will destroy the order of the ecosystem.
ライオンとトラは夜行性動物です。	Lions and tigers are nocturnal animals.
クジラは海で暮らしていますが、哺乳類です。	Whales live in the sea, but they are mammals.
カエルは両生類ですか、は虫類ですか?	Are frogs amphibians or reptiles?
昆虫が地球上の動物の90パーセント以上を占めています。	Insects make up more than 90 percent of the animals on Earth.

oxygen
酸素

hydrogen
水素

carbon
炭素

nitrogen
窒素

carbon dioxide (CO$_2$)
二酸化炭素

ozone layer
オゾン層

atmosphere
地球の大気

EARTH

ultraviolet rays [light]
紫外線

infrared rays [light]
赤外線

gas
気体

liquid
液体（の）

solid
固体（の）

rock
岩石、岩、石ころ

stone
石、石ころ

pebble
小石、砂利

* **sand** 砂　　* **soil** 土、土壌

* **mud** 泥　　* **mineral** 鉱物

USEFUL SENTENCES

水は水素と酸素で構成されています。	Water is composed of hydrogen and oxygen.
二酸化炭素は温室効果の主な原因と考えられています。	Carbon dioxide is considered the main cause of the greenhouse effect.
オゾン層の破壊を防がなければなりません。	The ozone layer should be prevented from being destroyed.
窒素と酸素が地球の大気の99パーセントを占めています。	Nitrogen and oxygen make up 99 percent of the Earth's atmosphere.
紫外線は人間の肌に有害です。	Ultraviolet rays are harmful to human skin.
水は、気体、液体、固体の状態で存在します。	Water exists in gaseous, liquid, and solid states.

4 環境問題

DL 16_05

environmental protection 環境保護
environmental problem 環境問題
environmental pollution 環境汚染
environmentalist, environmental activist 環境運動家

global warming 地球温暖化
greenhouse gas 温室ガス
greenhouse effect 温室効果

environment-friendly, eco-friendly
環境に優しい

climate change
気候変動

fossil fuel
化石燃料

USEFUL SENTENCES

環境汚染は人類にとって深刻な問題です。

Environmental pollution is a serious problem for humankind.

アル・ゴア元アメリカ副大統領は、環境運動家です。

Former U.S. Vice President Al Gore is an environmentalist.

地球の平均気温が高くなることが、地球温暖化です。

Global warming is the rise of the average global temperature.

温室効果を引き起こす気体を、温室効果ガスと呼ばれます。

Gases that cause the greenhouse effect are called greenhouse gases.

環境に優しい暮らし方について考えてみるべきです。

We have to think about living eco-friendly ways of life.

石炭、石油、天然ガスなどの化石燃料の利用が、大気汚染を引き起こしました。

The use of fossil fuels such as coal, oil and natural gas has caused air pollution.

green energy グリーンエネルギー
renewable energy 再生可能エネルギー
alternative energy 代替エネルギー

solar energy, solar power 太陽エネルギー
solar panel 太陽電池パネル
solar power generation 太陽光発電

wind power
風力エネルギー

wind farm
風力発電基地

forest conservation
森林保護

forest destruction
森林破壊

recycle
再生利用する

* **geothermal energy** 地熱エネルギー

USEFUL SENTENCES

環境保護のために、グリーンエネルギーを開発して利用すべきです。

We need to develop and use green energy to protect the environment.

そのアパートには太陽電池パネルが設置されています。

The apartment has solar panels.

地熱エネルギーは地下の熱水や地熱を利用したエネルギーです。

Geothermal energy is energy using hot groundwater or underground heat.

green energy, renewable energy, alternative energy
この3つの言葉はほぼ同じ意味で使われます。いずれも、環境破壊をもたらした既存の化石燃料エネルギーに代わる、環境に優しく再生利用が可能なエネルギーを指しています。
代表的なものとしては、太陽光エネルギー、太陽熱エネルギー、風力エネルギー、地熱エネルギー、水力エネルギー、水熱エネルギー、海洋エネルギー（海流、波）、バイオエネルギー、水素エネルギー、燃料電池、石炭を液化・ガス化したエネルギーなどがあります。

INDEX

H

S

ソ・ヨウンジョ

韓国外国語大学英語科、東国大学大学院演劇映画科を卒業。
英語教材出版分野で有益な英語学習コンテンツを開発。プロの翻訳家として、
英語圏の書籍と国際映画祭出品作の翻訳を行っている。
著書に『英会話の決定的単語』、『ディズニーOSTイングリッシュ』、
『ディズニージュニアイングリッシュ―冬の王国』、
『ディズニージュニアイングリッシュ―トイ・ストーリー4』などがある。

ピクトで学ぶ英会話必須単語3000+

発　　行　　日	2021年4月23日(初版)
著　　　　　者	ソ・ヨウンジョ

編　　　　　集	株式会社アルク 出版編集部
翻　　　　　訳	河井佳
校　　　　　正	Peter Branscombe、挙市玲子
デ　ザ　イ　ン	早坂美香(SHURIKEN Graphics)
ナレーション	Howard Colefield、Julia Yermakov
画　　　　　像	Shutter Stock
D　　T　　P	株式会社 創樹
印　刷　・　製　本	シナノ印刷株式会社
録　音　・　編　集	株式会社メディアスタイリスト

発　　行　　人	天野智之
発　　行　　所	株式会社アルク
	〒102-0073 東京都千代田区九段北4-2-6　市ヶ谷ビル
	Website: https://www.alc.co.jp/

地球人ネットワークを創る

アルクのシンボル
「地球人マーク」です。

落丁本、乱丁本は弊社にてお取り替えいたしております。
Webお問い合わせフォームにてご連絡ください。
https://www.alc.co.jp/inquiry/

Printed in Japan　PC: 7021010　ISBN: 978-4-7574-3682-4
BEYOND ENGLISH WORDS　By Suh Youngjo
Copyright © 2020 by Suh Youngjo First published in Korea in 2020
by Saramin Japanese translation rights arranged with Saramin through Shinwon Agency Co.
Japanse edition copyright © 2021 by ALC PRESS INC.

本書は韓国で刊行された『英会話の決定的単語』の日本語版です。原書で人名が韓国語になっているものや、
韓国独特の文化に関する表現は出版社の許可を得て日本風のものに変更しています。